FRED WHO?

Political Insider to Outsider

by
Fred Karger

with Steve Fiffer

TABLE OF CONTENTS

ACKNOWLEDGMENTS

I have been very fortunate in life, and the two big reasons for that are my parents, Jean and Bob Karger. They made me the man I am today. They instilled so many important values in me: helping others, loyalty, laughing, working hard, enjoying life, not taking no for an answer, and starting at the top.

My boss and political mentor, Bill Roberts, taught me so much as well: be courageous, get along with people, stay grounded, be tough, help those in need, analyze a problem and go tackle it. Bill always wanted to manage a presidential campaign, and I know he is somehow running mine. Robert F. Gentry is another mentor and role model who so inspired me when he became the first openly gay mayor in the U.S. in 1982. Bob helped me again, when I became out and active in 2006, by giving me the courage to be myself and take a stand.

Steve Fiffer, who contacted me about writing my memoir a year ago, has written another remarkable book. Thank you for your idea, brilliance, hand holding, and all you did to make *FRED WHO?* a wonderful read. Steve previously collaborated with former Secretary of State James A. Baker and civil rights lawyer Morris Dees on their autobiographies, so I'm in good company. In addition to Steve, this book would not have been possible without the efforts of Brad Mayo (graphic designer extraordinaire), Kate Sloan Fiffer (production manager/jack of all trades), and Maureen McNair and Nora Fiffer, who transcribed so many notes and videos. My attorney and friend Cary Davidson, whose superb work on my behalf is chronicled on the pages that follow, played an important role regarding book contracts. The excellent photographer Greg Powers of Washington, D.C., took the picture that graces the cover.

Thanks to so many friends and colleagues who shared past memories with Steve and me. These include Lee Stitzenberger, Kathy Lucker. Shane Miller, Russell Johnson, Rob Weinstein, Gary Wolfson, Bill Solomon, Jerry Blumberg, and my early campaign team Brian Wilson, Kevin Miniter, Rina Shah, and Matt Hammond. Special thanks to our filmmaker John Keitel, who has been documenting so much of what we're doing, and Danielle Avel, who has been so incredibly helpful and has become a wonderful friend.

Thank you also to my brother Dick for always being there for me and to Christine, the best sister-in-law possible. And to my other "big brother," Cousin Butch and his wife Nancy Karger, thank you both for being such wonderful inspirations and constant boosters of my activism. I love you all.

I would also like to thank and express my admiration to the hundreds of brave men and women, young and old, who have shared their hopes and dreams and trials and tribulations with me through emails, letters, Facebook, and other social media. The correspondence that precedes each chapter is only the tip of the iceberg. I run for president in large part because of them. And it does get better. I am so grateful to all those friends old and new who share these pages with me. My story is your story.

AUTHOR'S NOTE

This book covers a time frame of over sixty years. As others have acknowledged in their memoirs and autobiographies, it is difficult to remember everything exactly over such a lengthy period. I have tried my best to portray the events and conversations as accurately as possible—relying on conversations with certain of the principals to refresh my memory as well as contemporaneous media accounts. In two instances, I have changed the names of individuals to protect their privacy.

DEDICATION

For my parents Jean and Bob
and my mentor Bill Roberts.

PROLOGUE

"WOULDN'T THAT BE SOMETHING?"

People who meet me for the first time and hear my story often ask: "Were you always this way?"

"Yes," I tell them. "It's genetic. Couldn't change even if I wanted to."

I believe that. If you're looking for an explanation for my behavior, blame it on my DNA. That's what allowed me to talk my way onto Governor Nelson Rockefeller's campaign bus and former Vice President Hubert Humphrey's campaign plane. It's what led me to crash the stage at the Academy Awards as Charlie Chaplin was getting an honorary Oscar (and to walk arm-in-arm with Ann-Margret a few minutes later to shake Chaplin's hand). More recently, it's what enabled me to organize the boycott of a 1.7 billion dollar food conglomerate and to take on the Mormon Church for its insidious political practices.

What can I say? I was born with the chutzpah gene.

What's chutzpah? In his book, *The Joy of Yiddish*, humorist Leo Rosten described it as, "that quality enshrined in a man who, having killed his mother and father, throws himself on the mercy of the court because he is an orphan."

I prefer the stricter Hebrew translation: audacity. Sounds, er, presidential. Which makes perfect sense because here I am at the University of New Hampshire on a chilly day in March 2010, about to introduce myself to about forty members of the Alliance, a Lesbian, Gay, Bisexual, Transgender (LGBT) student organization. I've got an HD Video Flip Camera with me courtesy of a producer at CNN iReports, so the speech is recorded.

My name is Fred Karger. I'm crashing your event. I'm from California. I'm with an organization called Californians Against Hate, and I have spent my entire life since I was an adolescent in politics—first as a volunteer, then professionally with a company called the Dolphin Group in Los Angeles. I was there twenty-seven years until I retired in 2004. We ran political campaigns and we did a lot of corporate government affairs work. I'm what you'd call a political junkie.

I've been gay ever since I'm old enough to remember. I had a tough time dealing with it. I'm sixty years old now, but when I was a teenager and figuring everything out, it was a different era, and I struggled. I did everything I could to try and turn straight, including going to three psychiatrists. Fortunately all three of them said, "Sorry! Can't do that. But we'll work with you." Thank God they didn't say they could change me.

I lived in the closet for a long time, which was a very difficult experience. I was gay, I was partnered and everything, but politically it was very difficult to actually be out, so I had a double life and was okay with it, but it was … it took its toll.

I came out to my family in 1991 when I was forty-one. My parents were surprised, believe it or not. I'd told a few friends before that, and later I told the rest of my family and more friends. But in twenty-seven years, I only told a few people at work.

Obviously I wasn't an activist during that time. But about two years after I retired from the Dolphin Group, I took the plunge and got involved in the town where I live, Laguna Beach.

There was a great bar there called the Boom Boom Room that was the center of the gay community. A billionaire bought it and was getting ready to close it so he could develop the land it was on, and I decided, Okay, I'm going to jump into this thing.

I started an effort called "Save the Boom." Using a lot of what I'd learned in my political work over the years, I helped keep the Boom open an extra year. This got me a lot of publicity, national press and everything, particularly after I tried to involve Brad Pitt and George Clooney.

The experience was very traumatic for me. At fifty-six years old, I was suddenly out and gay for all to see. I had bottled this up for so long. Still, I think it was tremendously helpful and made me feel better. And I think it also kind of woke up a lot of other people who were in a similar situation.

Fifty-six years is a long time. When I first realized I was gay, there weren't really any role models. There were two pretty famous people who were presumed to be gay, but neither was out. One was Liberace. You know who he was? Very flamboyant entertainer. The other was Paul Lynde, a guy in a lot of sitcoms and the center square on the TV show, "Hollywood Squares." That was it.

Forty-plus years later a lot has changed. A lot of great people have come out. And the LGBT community has many wonderful allies now. Being gay is no big deal in so many areas.

But unfortunately that's not the case everywhere by any stretch of the imagination.

Take my state. As you know there was a measure on the 2008 ballot in California called Proposition 8. It sought to outlaw same sex marriage, which had previously been given the green light by the courts. Fresh from trying to save the Boom, I joined the campaign to preserve the right to marry like our straight brothers and sisters. I started an organization called Californians Against Hate. One of the first things we did was organize a boycott of one of the biggest donors who had helped to get Prop 8 on the ballot. His name is Doug Manchester and he owns the biggest hotel in San Diego, the Manchester Grand Hyatt. He gave $125,000 to defeat same sex marriage and gloated about it to the newspapers.

That got me pissed off, and I'm not a good guy to get pissed off. So I started a boycott of the hotel with UNITE HERE, Local 30, the hotel workers' union. It's now going on its second year. We just had a big success. The American Psychological Association announced it will honor the boycott. There have been about twenty-five major groups like this who have cancelled conventions and meetings at the hotel. Doug Manchester's own people estimate the hotel is losing about a million dollars a month just in convention business, so we've sent a very loud message to other donors that if you're going to give money to take away our civil rights, we may choose not to give you business, and our friends and allies might not also.

I've done three other boycotts. One was against Bolthouse Farms, a billion dollar-plus company that is one of the biggest carrot growers in the U.S. and has a line of upscale juices.

Eventually, Bolthouse's owners agreed to give LGBT organizations the same amount of money that founder William Bolthouse had given in support of Prop 8—$100,000. They've also done some really good diversity training.

I organized a second boycott against a family-owned business in Salt Lake City, Utah, that owns more than forty car dealerships in several states. The matriarch of the family had also given $100,000 in support of Prop 8. I went to Salt Lake to announce the boycott, and by the end of the afternoon I was in the company's offices discussing a settlement. Soon we had an agreement like the one with Bolthouse. They agreed to give at least $100,000 to LGBT organizations in Utah.

This kind of activity makes a lot of our national and state gay organizations nervous. We've never done this before. We've never boycotted major donors like this. But the San Diego boycott of Manchester's hotel has caught on. We've made some great strategic alliances with some unlikely partners like the unions.

So I've taken to this activism. After we were defeated on Prop 8, I stayed with it. I started looking at campaign spending reports and saw a trend. A huge amount of the $40 million raised in support of Prop 8 came from the Mormon Church and its members.

But the Church itself only reported $2,078. I knew that was low because they did every aspect of that campaign. So I filed a complaint with the California Fair Political Practices Commission, the ethics commission, and it announced an unprecedented investigation of the Mormon Church. Never been done before. We don't know what's happening with that, if the

Church is cooperating, but it certainly put them on notice that we're now watching them. They've been involved in thirty other states where same sex marriage was defeated.

As you know Maine had a similar proposition on the ballot in November 2009, called Question 1, to take away the recently passed gay marriage bill, just like what happened the year before in California. I looked at the first campaign finance report, and I noticed that the National Organization for Marriage (NOM) had given over $500,000, two-thirds of all the money raised, just as it had done early on in California. By now I knew it was a front group established by the Mormon Church to fight gay marriage everywhere. And so I asked for an investigation in Maine and charged NOM with money laundering. Along with a good lesbian friend I met during Prop 8 who has been helping me with research, I went up to Augusta and we testified in front of the Maine Commission on Governmental Ethics and Election Practices. And you know what? In dramatic fashion, after its own staff report recommended against an investigation, the commission voted three-two to investigate the National Organization for Marriage—which a month earlier had subpoenaed me in an attempt to silence me.

After California agreed to investigate the Mormon Church, NOM was trying to get California's campaign reporting laws eliminated and sued all state election officials in order to do so. A year later in response to another investigation, they sued the small state of Maine to intimidate it into dropping its investigation. What guts!

So I keep going back to Augusta to make sure that doesn't happen. I want NOM to know I'm watching. I'm a strong believer *and practitioner of following through. If you're going to start something, you should be prepared to finish it.*

Which in a way is what brings me here. After Maine, I went back to California and started thinking about a new, bigger undertaking: running for president. I haven't decided quite yet, but I am seriously thinking of becoming the first openly gay candidate to run for president in the history of the country.

If I do this, you're going to see a lot of me in New Hampshire. I'm going to follow the Obama mold—organize younger voters, register them, and have them active in the campaign. Your group would be very crucial in this whole effort because the gay-straight alliances here and at the other colleges in and around New Hampshire will be instrumental to what I do.

I've saved the best for last. If I decide to run for president, it will be as a Republican. Wouldn't that be something? Entering the caucuses and primaries as a candidate for the nomination of a party that hasn't exactly embraced gay equality? But don't forget, the Republican Party is the party of Abraham Lincoln. You guys may be too young to remember, but there was a time when the Republicans led the way in civil rights and equality and the Democrats did not; they were the stonewallers.

So this is who I am, what I've done, and what I'm thinking of doing. As I said, I'm still just starting the process. But I can tell you one thing: if I move forward, it won't be half-hearted.

Thanks so much for giving me the opportunity to speak to you. I have a feeling this won't be the last time we're together.

And, it hasn't been. As I write this I've visited sixteen times and spent at least three months in New Hampshire over the last year and a half.

When I went into that meeting with those students, I really wasn't sure if I wanted to run for president. I've been in politics my whole life, so I knew it sounded preposterous. Never held elective office. No name recognition. No funding.

But something happened in that room with those kids. As I spoke, I could see they were enthralled with what I was thinking of doing. My story resonated with them. They've grown up in a better, more accepting time than I did. But they know what it's like to be on the outside, to live a lie, to be worried if your parents or friends would still love you if they knew the truth. I knew at that moment I had to do this.

When I started my Proposition 8 activism, I stated, "I'm doing this for younger people. I don't want them to go through what I went through, and I had it a lot better than most. It was terrible, but I'm fine now, and in a position to make a difference." The same goes for a run for the presidency.

Chutzpah? Yes. But if I'm not mistaken, only a few years ago, a long shot candidate for president wrote and spoke of the virtues of and the need for audacity.

On my next trip to New Hampshire, I passed out T-shirts that read FRED WHO?

My job in that state and on the pages that follow here is to answer that question ... and more. Who am I? Why am I running? What do I stand for?

I hope you'll keep reading to learn the answers. I don't think you'll be bored. It's been an interesting campaign and an interesting life. On the pages that follow, you'll meet the people who made it so interesting: from Rock Hudson to Ronald Reagan. From Lynda "Wonder Woman" Carter to Barry Goldwater. From Cesar Chavez to Lee Atwater. And more. I've been a part of nine presidential campaigns, and more Senate, gubernatorial, congressional, and state and local campaigns than I can count. I've represented the tobacco industry and worked with environmental groups. I've made friends with the hotel workers union and enemies of the Church of Jesus Christ of Latter-day Saints (Mormons). I've supported Hillary Clinton and gone after Mitt Romney and Mike Huckabee. I've been featured in one of the most famous commercials of all time, and I've had my life threatened. And perhaps most interesting of all, I led a dual existence for the first fifty-six years of my life.

Fred,

I wanted to thank you for expressing your stances on many social issues. I am 17 years old and I will turn 18 before the next election. I am "fiscally conservative" but "socially liberal." It's nice to have a Republican candidate that's not afraid to separate from the pack of the traditional conservatives and express his/her real beliefs. I especially like your stance on Gay marriage/rights. For me, treating heterosexuals and homosexuals a certain way should not be about political or religious ideology; it should be about being moral and ethical and treating them equally. I am gay, although I am not "out" to my friends and family. Being a gay Republican is kinda tough, but we still need someone in the White House that supports LGBT rights. Again, I wanted to thank you, and best of luck with the campaign.

Brian

CHAPTER ONE

"IT'S DON'S FAULT."

It's early September 1971. Tomorrow I'm supposed to leave our home outside Chicago for Denver and my senior year of college. My older brother Dick will be heading in the other direction. He's taken a position at an investment bank in New York City. And so on the eve of our departures, my parents have organized a small family dinner. My mom's sister Doris and her family are here. My mom's brother Buddy is not.

Buddy's not exactly an outcast, but he's the guy in the family that everyone likes to make fun of. He sells insurance. Never married, but seen around town in the company of very attractive women, some of them showgirls. Despite the fact that he's sometimes the butt of jokes, I like him. Maybe it's because folks have always said I remind them of him. Or maybe it's because I know something they don't know.

After dinner the eight of us are in the den when the phone rings. We all hear my mother scream, "Oh God, Buddy's dead!"

He's killed himself, overdosed on pills and alcohol. He was forty-two.

Why? No one is sure. His three-word suicide note only heightens the mystery: "It's Don's fault."

The only Don we know is a guy who had worked for my father. He's one of Buddy's friends. What could have happened?

Here's what I know that nobody else in the family knows: Uncle Buddy was gay.

Here's how I know it: On my very first trip to a gay bar in Chicago when I was 19, I saw Buddy. Fortunately, he didn't see me. I hid behind some people and quickly left. I never told a soul.

And now, two years later, he's dead. Killed himself. Growing up, everybody had always said that I looked just like him. If only they knew how alike we were. *So*, I think as I lie awake in my bed, the tears streaming down my face, *this is my destiny*. Some day, just like Uncle Buddy, I'm not going to be able to live with my secret anymore. It's only a matter of time.

***

If you had known me back then or in the twenty-one years of my life leading up to that night, you might have thought I was a little goofy, the class clown, the guy who crashed political and charity events, but you wouldn't have known I was gay or that I was in despair. In fact, when I describe my childhood, I also use four words: "Leave It to Beaver."

My parents, Jean and Bob Karger, were June and Ward Cleaver. My older brother Dick was Wally, the cool jock and ladies' man. And I was the Beave, lovable, but often in trouble. We lived in a comfortable two-story, four-bedroom house in Glencoe, a suburb on the lake about twenty miles north of Chicago. I kid you not, we had the exact same refrigerator that the Cleavers had on the television show.

Like June, Jean was a stay-at-home mom. If I tell you my mother was a Foreman, that probably means nothing to you. In their day, however, the Foremans were one of the most affluent

Jewish families in Chicago. Gerhardt Foreman, a German immigrant, had established the first Foreman Bank in Chicago in 1862, and on the eve of the Great Depression its reorganized successor, still controlled by the family, was the third biggest bank in the city. It was housed in the center of the financial district at 33 N. LaSalle in a new forty-story skyscraper the family had built and named the Foreman Bank Building.

My mom, born in 1918, grew up on what was called the "Foreman Estate" in Highland Park, another suburb north of Chicago. She lived in a big house situated on six acres on the shore of Lake Michigan. The family had thirteen servants—all white Europeans—including upstairs and downstairs maids, cooks, and two nurses. They had several cars and, of course, a chauffeur. They lived like royalty and were often featured in the society columns.

If the Depression hadn't come along, I probably would be in a position now to finance my own campaign in Meg Whitman dollars. But in 1931 the bank had to close its doors. The Foremans didn't lose everything, but they took a huge hit. Luckily for them my mother's maternal grandmother still had some money. She helped the family move from the estate into a beautiful two-story apartment in Chicago's fancy Gold Coast area. It was a come-down, but they still lived well. Although they had to let most of the servants go, the Foremans still had a nurse and a cook and a few maids.

My mom finished high school in the city at Francis Parker, a private school, then went off to Briarcliff, a somewhat hoity-toity women's junior college in Westchester County outside New York City. Eventually she went to art school in Chicago. Although she never worked outside the home, she volunteered—always twice a week, one day with mentally disabled adults, and one day at a preschool. Years later she traded work at the preschool to volunteer at the North Shore Senior Center. She did this her entire life. This was a legacy from her parents that she passed down to me.

My parents met at the twenty-first birthday party of a wealthy cousin. I came to know him well growing up. We used to go swimming at his magnificent estate in Glencoe. He became a well-known designer, and was married with children. Nobody ever talked about his sexual orientation in my presence. As a kid I never suspected he was gay. Members of that generation felt they had to get married to keep their secrets. Years later, I heard that he was in the closet.

I only mention this because when I was in my twenties, my parents and I stayed at his beautiful home in Palm Springs, California. My mother was putting away some things in his closet and came across a bunch of caftans. She looked at me, shook her head, and said, "Doesn't that just make you sick." These are not the words a young man with his own gay secret wants to hear from his mother. It was a throw away line, but stuck with me. It suggested how my parents might handle things if I shared that secret—so back it went into the vault for another twenty years.

But back to my parents' meeting in 1940. My father's family, like my mother's, had also emigrated from Germany. The Kargers had settled in Michigan's Upper Peninsula before moving to Chicago, where they had a fairly successful meat company, S. Karger and Sons. In Chicago my grandfather, Sam Karger, met and married my grandmother, whose family had considerable wealth from their department store, Rothschild's, and extensive real estate holdings.

The German-Jewish community in Chicago was tight-knit, if not insular. Lake Shore Country Club in Glencoe was one of the centers of that community, and the Kargers and Foremans were each members. June and Ward's, I mean Jean and Bob's, parents not only knew each other, they were related. My parents were fifth cousins.

Because my father was seven years older than my mother, they hadn't met before that birthday party. The Dad I knew had a wry sense of humor and could play wonderful practical jokes, but for the most part he was as straight-laced as they come. I do suspect he raised some hell as a teenager, though. He attended four different private high schools in four years. Then he enrolled at the University of Arizona.

When the Depression came, he dropped out of college to save his parents' money. He came back to Chicago and joined the family business, a brokerage house called Rothschild and Co., founded by his father Sam and Sam's brother-in-law Jesse Rothschild in 1908. (My paternal grandmother was a Rothschild, but not related to *the* Rothschilds.)

Unfortunately, I never knew either of my grandfathers. One passed away before I was born, the other when I was six months old. I grew up hearing a lot about them and remember this about Sam: He didn't believe in buying anything. He leased or rented everything. He had a chauffeur, too, but he never owned his car or a house. Maybe that's why he survived the Depression.

My parents married in April of 1941. After Pearl Harbor, my father tried to enlist in the Navy. He was turned down because he had flat feet, but the Army accepted him. Just before he was to go overseas, while stationed in Paso Robles, California, he jumped into a foxhole during a drill and broke his back. Bad as that was, it probably saved his life. Most of his unit got wiped out in the Pacific. My mother moved out to California to be with him, and he stayed stateside in the Army until the war was almost over. Then they came back to Chicago.

My parents moved into an apartment on the Gold Coast a few blocks from my mother's parents and then to Hyde Park on the city's south side. Dick was born in 1946, and I followed in January of 1950. Six months later we moved to Glencoe and the house where my parents would live for the next 28 years.

When I was growing up, Glencoe—population 10,500—was the suburb on the North Shore that attracted the more well-to-do Jewish families moving on up from the city. Indeed, in those days some of the nearby communities did not welcome Jews with open arms. Glencoe also had the only sizable black population on the North Shore.

For most of my classmates, "idyllic" might best describe our childhoods in the 1950s and early 1960s. We rode our bikes everywhere—to school, the Good Humor ice cream truck, the soda fountain, the barbershop, the deli. We never locked those Schwinns, and our parents never locked the house.

The elementary school field hosted softball in the spring and summer, touch football in the fall, and, weather permitting, ice hockey in the winter. In junior high, we had parties almost every weekend at which a teenager from Harvey's, the local record shop, spun 45s by the Four Seasons and the Beach Boys and Ricky Nelson and Lesley Gore. We danced the cha-cha, jitterbug, twist, and every now and then a close one. Occasionally, the outside world invaded. John F. Kennedy was assassinated when we were in 8th grade. Blessedly, a few months later, the Beatles arrived in New York.

How idyllic? Our eighth grade 1964 Central School class holds reunions at least once every five years. This past year about sixty classmates—fully one-fourth of us—gathered for a joint 60th birthday celebration.

Idyllic and yet.... When you start to realize you are different than your friends—that you are attracted to boys instead of girls—what are you supposed to do? Who are you supposed to talk to?

I started having those feelings around fifth or sixth grade, the same time when my straight guy friends—everybody else, I assumed—were having similar feelings about girls. I had a huge crush on one boy a year ahead of me in school, Johnny Lee. I used to call his house all the time and when he got on the line, I'd just hang up. I felt terribly guilty doing this, but then I'd go to school and be all right the next day.

At overnight camp, when I was twelve years old, I had what you might call my first gay experience in a tent with a couple of older campers. That was largely the extent of my junior high school forays into homosexuality. In high school, I'd get together with a special friend or two and we'd just play around a little. At the same time I was dating girls ... and going farther with them than any of the guys I was with.

Why the girls? I thought this was the right thing to do. I didn't want anybody to be suspicious of me. I was hoping I could change. And there are worse things you can do as a teenager than making out or more with a cute girl.

When I see myself in home movies from this period, I think I look effeminate. I can't believe no one suspected I was gay. But then again, no one was looking for that kind of thing in those days. I don't recall ever hearing the word "gay" back then, and don't remember thinking of myself as "queer"—just different, I guess.

My self-esteem during these years was about the same as my grade point average. Pretty low. Except for math, school didn't engage me. And this was despite the fact that Glencoe had a terrific school system and my high school, New Trier, was and still is rated among the best in the country.

(In making educational reform a central plank in my campaign platform, I am most interested in finding new ways to interest our young people so that they'll want to stay in school and be able to learn better. Interestingly, when I recently met with the head of a foundation that invests heavily in education, he didn't like one of my questions: How can we make school more fun.? *Fun?* he replied. *Fun? School's not supposed to be fun!* Maybe I should have said "more interesting" instead of "fun," but we've got over a million kids dropping out of high school every year. Why not make it fun so they'll stay?)

New Trier has given us numerous luminaries in the two areas that have always interested me most: politics and acting. Among the alum: Donald Rumsfeld, Rahm Emanuel, Charlton Heston, and Ann-Margret and Rock Hudson. The latter two were several years ahead of me in high school, but our paths would cross in Los Angeles.

My brother was a star, if not a luminary, during his high school years. His success in the classroom and in sports—he was starting varsity quarterback—didn't help my self-image. Teachers, camp counselors, family friends, maybe even my parents, expected me to be as athletic and smart as Dick was. But I wasn't. It was hard to live in his shadow. (We've grown close over the years, but we weren't very close then. He was more like my dad—the self-driven hard worker. I was more like my mom—the spontaneous people person.)

In high school I was on the swim team for three years and acted in a few plays, but I also goofed off quite a bit. Still, I had a lot of friends and found a niche for myself as a funny man.

Recently, one friend from childhood told me he thought the following incident captured who I was in those days: In addition to our weekend parties in junior high, we all went to a more formal weekly class where we learned dance steps and manners. At the beginning of each class, we lined up to shake hands with our two teachers. "Hello, Mr. Giordano. Hello, Miss Livingston." One day I went through the line with one of those vibrating hand buzzers and scared the bejesus out of Mr. G. I was thrown out of dancing school that day. (So maybe I was more Eddie Haskell than the Beave!)

I did have a serious passion: politics. My parents were both Rockefeller Republicans—social moderates—another legacy they passed on to me. My dad was the precinct captain, and I would often accompany him to the Glencoe train station, where we'd pass out literature for our candidates to commuters. I'd just go up to them fearlessly with a flier touting Eisenhower or whoever was running at the time. Who's going to turn down a 6- or an 8-year-old kid?

When I was fourteen, I worked on two campaigns—Nelson Rockefeller for President and Charles Percy for Governor. For Rocky, I took the train into Chicago and helped man the phone banks in the basement of the old Sherman House hotel. For Percy, another moderate, I rode my bike about six miles to his headquarters in Kenilworth. There I'd do everything from sweeping floors to running the postage machine.

Not too long ago I told this story to a reporter. "Why would a 14-year-old kid work in politics?" she asked.

"Well, I never thought about it," I said. Then as I reflected, I thought, *well, they welcomed me.* I wasn't great in school. I was not a good athlete. I was trying to figure everything out, I guess. But I'd go into a political campaign office and there was no judgment. It was a safe, wonderful place to be and I kind of shined at that. When I think about it, I realize I've been in dozens and dozens of campaigns, and I don't ever remember a 14- or 16-year-old kid just coming into the office.

Rockefeller lost the 1964 nomination to Barry Goldwater (who would figure prominently in my life twenty years later). Percy lost the governor's race to Otto Kerner. But just as they were undaunted, so was I.

By 1966, when Percy was running for the U.S. Senate, I had my driver's license. I'd go to the headquarters and then they might send me out to pick up or deliver something. I even got to go to the Percy mansion on the lake a few times—once just a week or so before their daughter Valerie was murdered in her bedroom in the middle of the night. (To this day, the murder remains unsolved. For many on the North Shore, this was a watershed event, the end of innocence. We began locking our doors at night or when we went out. Years later, I'd have the opportunity to work in political campaigns with families who had lost loved ones to murder. As I'll explain later, it was both sobering and uplifting and it led to one of the most infamous commercials of all time.)

In 1968, my senior year in high school, I again worked on the Rockefeller for President campaign. When Rocky came to town, my friend Wendy Nagle and I went to hear him speak. I wore a sport coat because I figured I might be able to talk my way into meeting him. Sure enough, through a combination of chutzpah and the luck of being in the right place at the right time, we ended up in the elevator with him. After snapping some pictures, we followed him out of the hotel right onto his campaign bus.

The bus drove all over the city. Rockefeller walked the aisle, working the press. I kept hoping we'd run into somebody I knew at one of the stops, but we never did.

This was one of my earliest and most successful crashes. As you'll see throughout the book, crashing has always been a serious hobby, and I've always been quite good at it. Maybe I couldn't break through a defensive line like my brother could, but I could break through a security line with the best of 'em.

Another adventure from this time period: My friend Rob Weinstein and I decided to crash The Crystal Ball, the greatest charity gala of the season in Chicago. It was being held in a big hotel—the Conrad Hilton—and my parents were going.

Rob and I went to the hotel's uniform room, told them our sizes, and *voila*! We were now Crystal Ball waiters. We just wandered around taking in all the dressed-up people dining and dancing. Eventually I went up to my mother and in a Spanish accent said, "Excuse me, ma'am, would you like some tea?"

She had her back turned to me and was eating her dessert. She turned around and said, "How do you know I drink tea?" Then she started to laugh. My cousin, Maggie Block, was also at the Ball. She apparently told her publicist the tale, and the next day the *Chicago Tribune*'s society column ran it—one of my earliest press mentions.

I credit my success at crashing to both the chutzpah gene *and* the gay gene. I think gay people are often a lot more clever than our straight counterparts. We've got to be creative to lead our double lives, to come up with stories, to boldly pretend we're someone we aren't.

As high school came to a close, I was pretty sure I knew who I was—didn't like it—but knew. Before going off to college, I raised the stakes. Driving home from Chicago one day, I was suddenly possessed to stop at a park near Northwestern University in Evanston. I walked around, looking for what I'm not sure. But soon I found it, or him, a guy sunbathing in a Speedo bathing suit.

Nervous as can be, I looked at him. He looked back. I went to my car and waited. He went to his car and I followed him. We pulled over and talked in his car.

We were supposed to meet the next day back at the park. I was so scared that I didn't sleep. But before the appointed hour, my father called and said that his two messengers were out and that he needed me to report to duty at his office. And so, I stood the guy up.

If there's a silver lining to this story, it's that I ended up working for my dad that summer as a messenger. In the course of my daily rounds, I often had to go to the First National Bank. There, at the savings bonds window, a good-looking blond guy caught my eye. I'd walk past him at least twice a day, but I never had any reason to get in his line. Finally, I got up my nerve and with seventeen hard-earned dollars bought a $25 savings bond.

My crush had noticed me, too. He invited me to come over to his apartment that night. When I got there, he dumped me off on his roommate. I was a little disappointed, but by evening's end I'd had my first real experience. The guys introduced me to some other gay people and told me about the bars in town.

I was now a member of the club.

Mr. Karger,

I just wanted to thank you for your work to make society a better place for all people. You and others like you help pave the way towards a bright future and have helped me realize that I can be the person I was meant to be.

I grew up in a fundamentalist Christian home. My father is a minister and throughout my entire childhood, I was indoctrinated into a very narrow view of the world, one where gays were seen as "sinful" and "disgusting." I never really fit in as a child and I always had nagging questions in the back of my head about religion, sexuality and life.

Fast forward to age 21 and I've now accepted that I am gay and have also left religion altogether. My parents don't know (because they're helping pay for college) that I'm gay and an atheist and it can be difficult and quite stressful to keep my true self hidden for the time being.

However, people like you, who fight for the rights of all, make me realize that I can live in a country where I can be free and unashamed of who I am. The past year has been the most liberating time in my life.

So, thank you for all you do. Keep fighting the good fight and striving for truth.

M

CHAPTER TWO

"YOU SHOULD BE AN ACTOR."

It's April 1972, six months after Uncle Buddy's suicide. My double life is still a secret. I've had a couple of steady girlfriends and, I guess, dated a guy. I've gone to plenty of straight bars with my Phi Sigma Delta fraternity brothers. And I've gone to gay bars where nobody knows my name. In a few months, I'll have my degree in Speech Communications.

My parents are expecting me to come back to Chicago after graduation and work in the family stock brokerage business, Rothschild and Co. I have no idea what I want to do when I graduate or where I want to live. More important, more troubling: I can't imagine maintaining my secret if I return to my hometown. The chance of running into a friend or family member when out with a guy is terrifying.

But I'm not thinking about that now. Following in the family tradition of volunteering, I am currently working on our fraternity's annual fundraiser—a dance marathon, our most ambitious undertaking of all our yearly events. Allan Dorfman, the wealthy, and let's say "well-connected," father of one of my fraternity brothers has made us an offer we can't refuse. If we can get a Hollywood star to appear at the event, he will fly him or her back and forth at no cost on the private jet of the union pension fund he heads. The Lear Jet used to belong to Frank Sinatra, so it is a nice one.

I love a challenge. For most of my life, I've been talking my way into all sorts of places I should never be allowed. Can I get up-close-and-personal with a celebrity and persuade him or her to come to our dance marathon in Denver?

A fraternity brother and I will fly out to Los Angeles during Spring Break in search of our celebrity. Our trip happens to coincide with the Academy Awards. Maybe, by hook or by crook, I'll be able to score a couple of tickets.

We'll do more than that. I'll end up on stage with Charlie Chaplin and other megastars in front of Hollywood's elite and millions of television viewers around the world. I'll hobnob with Alfred Hitchcock, Groucho Marx, Raquel Welch, Jack Lemmon, and Ann-Margret. I'll meet a high-powered personal manager who will tell me he can get me into show business. The trip will be the high point of my college years ... and eventually the occasion of my near undoing.

***

Those college years began in September of 1968. My high school grades were less than stellar. But thanks to an above average score on the math SAT, I was able to get into my "stretch school." In addition to (or in spite of!) offering an academic challenge the University of Denver (DU) appealed to me because it allowed freshmen to have cars on campus. (What a way to pick a school, huh?)

Denver was a "Greek" school, with fifteen or so fraternities, two of which were Jewish. Bent on assimilating, I flirted with joining a "Gentile house." In the end, however, I joined three of my Jewish best friends from high school and several other freshmen from the North Shore in Phi Sigma Delta. Phi Sig actively rushed me, which was really flattering. Our house on Columbine Street was the center of my social life—at least my public social life—for the next four years.

Being Jewish didn't present any problems in college. Being out as a Republican, however, could be problematic. In November, less than two months after arriving on campus, I was in a distinct minority supporting Richard Nixon over Hubert Humphrey for the presidency.

When Nixon came to Denver on a campaign swing, I went to see him with a couple of friends. I was in the right place at the right time and as he moved quickly through the crowd with his wife, Pat, I slipped him a check made payable to Richard Nixon for $1.00, palming it like you would tip a restaurant host. He stopped and made a point of thanking me and saying how nice it was to have the support of young people. It was meant to be a goof, but I got great photos of the future president and a thank you letter three days later.

The war in Vietnam was at its peak between 1968 and 1972. So was the anti-war movement. At DU, like many schools across the country, word of the U.S.'s secret incursion into Cambodia and then the subsequent May 4, 1970, killing of innocents at Kent State University in Ohio triggered campus-wide protest. Students demonstrated against the government and against the university's decision to stay open during this turbulent period. Soon tents had been pitched in a place called Carnegie Green. Shanties were built, too, and the site was dubbed Woodstock West.

The scene was peaceful. There were speeches. There was music. There were campfires. And there were drugs. (Like fellow students and other politicians, I smoked pot in college. Even took some diet pills—which were legal back then and pretty common— to lose weight, study for exams, and for confidence.).

As a moderate member of the GOP, I was torn by Vietnam and by the protests. Initially, I was certainly more hawkish than the vast majority of my friends. By 1970 and the end of sophomore year, I had become more of a dove—in part because I didn't want to be in conflict with everybody else and in part because the war just didn't seem winnable. (My opposition to the recent wars in Iraq and Afghanistan has nothing to do with pleasing anybody. Rather, I've concluded they are, like Vietnam, unwinnable quagmires that cost far too much in terms of lives, injuries, and money.)

Some people forget that the Selective Service System's draft did not end until 1973. Most of the soldiers who died for this country in Vietnam did not enlist; they were drafted. Blessed with parents who could afford to send me to college (where I could take advantage of the student deferment), I was off to Europe instead of Southeast Asia after my sophomore year ended. My travel buddy was Rob Weinstein, a good friend from childhood. We would fly on a DU charter from New York to London and then drive around the continent for a couple of months.

Before departing, we stayed in Manhattan for a few days. On the eve of our flight, my mom called. She'd received a notice that I'd flunked out of school; my grade point average had fallen below the magic 2.0 level.

I had only myself to blame. I'd spent much more time the last two years having fun rather than studying. Also, thinking I was destined to join my father's business, I had started out as a business major. I had no interest in school, and my grades showed it. So after doing poorly in the School of Business, I switched my major to communications.

Mom said she wasn't going to call me because she didn't want to spoil my trip. Fortunately another good friend of mine whom she'd called for advice, Bill Solomon, had persuaded her to give me the news. "Maybe Fred can do something about it," Bill said.

Yes. The next day I was on pay phones all over New York (no cell phones in 1970), trying to find at least one professor who would raise one of my grades so I could reach 2.0. In between lunch with my Uncle John at the Harvard Club and going to the taping of a game show, I managed to track down all four of my professors. All said no, except Dr. Case, my speech/communications professor, whom I tracked down at a conference in Boulder, Colorado. He agreed to change the D he had given me to a B if I wrote a paper! As the van to take us to the airport was waiting, I got the news. Crisis averted—although my good-sport father had to work out the final arrangements.

Funny, isn't it? My parents proved themselves to be incredibly supportive when I screwed up—they were always there for me—but I couldn't imagine asking for their support in dealing with something over which I had no control: my sexual orientation.

And I did need support. I was trying my hardest to be like the rest of my fraternity brothers: partying and dating girls, and sleeping with them. But I was also walking dangerously close to the wild side. I tried to ignore my attraction to men, but couldn't.

Frequently I'd go on a date with a girl and drop her off early, feigning I was tired or something. And then? There were a couple of gay bars in Denver. Fake ID in hand, I'd go to them with great angst. Often, I'd meet people and go home with them. Then I'd come back to my house feeling so terrible that I would take an hour-long shower. Hoped it might wash away the shame, but it didn't.

I was always so scared I'd be seen in a bar, or walking to my car. But during my college years, I only ran into one person I knew—my Phi Sig little bróther of all people. It was actually nice to know that I was not the only one.

I'm often asked if friends and family ever unwittingly made derogatory references about gays in my presence. Outside of my mother's off-hand remark about the caftans in my cousin's closet, I can't really recall any. I was never put in the position of having to "go along with the guys" as they did any bashing or bullying or teasing, because I never heard such bashing. But I didn't need anybody else to tell me it was wrong to be attracted to men. I felt that way myself.

Having almost flunked out, I was put on academic probation my junior year. Students on probation had to agree to see a school psychiatrist at the health center. I had never been to one—never even thought about it. Our family was not the kind that relied on shrinks for answers. You worked it out on your own.

I still remember that first visit. The psychiatrist said, "Tell me about your mother," and I just burst into tears. Then he said, "Tell me about your father," and I burst into tears.

I told him about my attraction to men. We didn't resolve anything, but for the very first time I had someone to open up to. It was a huge breakthrough for me because of the secret I was keeping.

When I went back home on break, I asked my parents if I could see a psychiatrist. My father—the last person in the world to believe in psychiatry—said, "Sure."

My physician in Denver gave me three names. "It's gotta be a good fit," he said. "So go to each one once and see what you think. If you don't like any of those three, I'll give you three more."

That's what I did. At each meeting, I told the psychiatrist that I was gay, then watched his reaction. Then I said, "I would like to change." Each of the three said politely, but firmly, "You can't do that, but I can work with you."

I'd thought that I could be "cured." I am so grateful that each responded that way. It sure made me feel a lot better.

I went back seven or eight times to the doctor with whom I had the best rapport. We talked about coming to terms with my sexuality and other issues, too. Then he dismissed me. I didn't leave whole, but I felt much better for having had the opportunity to pour my heart out.

There was another reason for feeling better about myself. His name was Dan Brewster. He'd gone to New Trier and had received an MBA from Northwestern. He was great looking and blond, so sexy. The All-American Boy, it seemed.

We met in a gay bar in Chicago.

At twenty-six, Dan was five years older than I was. He lived in a beautiful apartment on Lake Shore Drive, the "ultimate bachelor pad," and he worked at the Leo Burnett advertising agency as an account executive. He came from a good family; his father was treasurer of a major Fortune 500 company. *Wow*. I didn't think there were gay people like this around. If you could be gay and be like Dan, then being gay was okay by me.

I'd met others up to this point, but I guess Dan was my first love, the guy who showed me the way. We would dance together. Remember the Pointer Sisters' song, "Respect Yourself"? When we danced to that, he would look directly into my eyes and sing along. He knew the problems I was having and wanted me to heed the anthem's message. They played that song in clubs a lot.

This relationship was what I needed at age twenty-one. More than any conversation with a psychiatrist, it helped me deal with all of my hang-ups and guilt and shame. We had the best time together. Once, I even snuck home from college for the weekend. I gave the Denver people some excuse, and I didn't even tell my family. The idea of flying home without telling your parents was unheard of.

As helpful as Dan and the psychiatrists were, I was still a mess when I went back to Denver for my senior year. Uncle Buddy had killed himself. Toss in some diet pills and the fact that I had some extra spending money thanks to Buddy's life insurance that he split between his four nephews, and I was primed for trouble.

Yes, I did okay academically, actually kind of shined in speech communications, interpersonal communications, and mass communications. And yes, I had a steady girlfriend. And yes, I had some extracurricular activities.

Rob Weinstein and I did a radio show on DU's radio station. It was called the "Krackers and Cheese Trivia Hour." Listeners called in weird questions and we tried to answer them humorously. We patterned ourselves after the successful comedy duo, Rowan and Martin. As Frank Krackers, I played the straight man to Rob's Rodney Cheese.

But I was still pushing the envelope.

Some of that pushing was harmless. Friends in tow, I led the crashing of dinners and balls at hotels like the Plaza in New York and the Hilton in Denver. We'd dress appropriately, talk our way in, and have good fun mixing and mingling and coming up with stories about why we were there.

Some of the pushing was edgier. I'd talk my way into an office (or sneak in) and pocket a memento to commemorate the success. Maybe a business card or notepad that I could use in a future exploit. Nothing particularly valuable. A youthful indiscretion. But still wrong.

Which brings me back to the trip to Los Angeles in April 1972. My fraternity brother and I are both still haunted by this episode, so for purposes of this story I will give him the pseudonym Dave.

Dave and I arrived in L.A. in the midst of Academy Award fever. Looking for the stars, we went to the Beverly Hills Hotel. There I met a photographer whom I assumed to be gay. He told us that Marshall Field IV, the department store heir and publisher of the *Chicago Sun Times*, and Bailey K. Howard, the former chairman of Field Enterprises, were throwing a big pre-Oscars party at a restaurant called the Bistro. "But you'll never get in," he said. "It's impossible."

That's all I needed to hear.

The photographs tell the story. In one, I'm with a dour Alfred Hitchcock and his wife. In another, I'm with a hip Hugh Hefner and his girlfriend, the Playmate Barbi Benton. And in a third, I'm with one of my heroes, Groucho Marx.

The only disappointing part of the evening was that we didn't finagle any tickets to the Oscar ceremony. But I had a plan for that, too. Here we have to flash back almost a year.

During the summer of 1971, I had visited Andy Bresler, a high school friend who had moved to New York. At that time "The Tonight Show" was based in Manhattan. On a lark we showed up at NBC Studios in Rockefeller Center, and ended up getting the last two seats available.

As we settled in, host Johnny Carson's announcer/sidekick Ed McMahon came out. "We're going to come out to the audience tonight. Who does impersonations?" Of course I raised my hand, then ticked off a whole slew of celebrities in my repertoire.

I had sold myself well, I guess, because when the show started, Joey Bishop—guest hosting for Johnny—came straight up to me in the audience. For almost four minutes, I did my thing. Several Jonathan Winters characters. Cary Grant, Jimmy Stewart. I was a pushy 21-year–old, even suggesting we turn the bit into "Stump the Audience," a take-off of the old "Tonight Show" staple,

"Stump the Band." I did Jack Benny, and Bishop countered with Benny's valet Rochester (Eddie Anderson). Many of my friends around the country saw me; back then, everybody watched "The Tonight Show."

The next day Andy and I went back to NBC so I could buy the kinescope (this was before video) of the show. (It's on YouTube now: http://www.youtube.com/watch?v=2PbO-cg3hDE). While there, I found a few NBC business cards and stationery as a souvenir.

As luck would have it, NBC was televising the Academy Awards. I had the business cards with me in Los Angeles. Doing another imitation—this time of an NBC executive—I called the Academy a day or two before the broadcast and said something to the effect of, "We've got two young men out from New York and they need some credentials. They'd like to watch the rehearsal." *Sure*, was the reply. *Tell them to come over now.*

We hurried over to the Dorothy Chandler Pavilion, where we were each given a white badge. We learned badges were color-coded to indicate where you could and couldn't go. White allowed you to go everywhere, including backstage.

Backstage! That's where I was on Oscar night, dressed in an outrageous blue denim tux, flowered dress shirt, and bow tie as big as a kite. It wasn't "gay." It was the seventies. I thought I was "stylin'," but I looked a little ridiculous.

Host Jack Lemmon and bombshell Raquel Welch each posed for pictures with me. When it was time for the legendary Charlie Chaplin to receive his honorary award, Dave and I were off stage. The call came for all winners and presenters to go on stage.

I looked at Dave and said, "Let's go." Over his objection, we went out on stage and joined Lemmon, all of the evening's presenters, nominees and winners, including best actress Jane Fonda (for "Klute") and best actor Gene Hackman (for the top movie, "The French Connection"). We positioned ourselves on the risers in the middle of all the stars.

When Chaplin came out, the entire audience leapt to its feet for what turned out to be a three or four minute ovation. There has never been an Academy Awards moment quite like that. Screams of "BRAVO" and thunderous applause is all we heard.

After Chaplin's short acceptance speech, everyone on the risers moved down to pay him homage. Ann-Margret (a nominee for best supporting actress) was on the riser next to me. Everybody was pairing off. She looked around and grabbed my arm and I escorted her. I remember telling her that I went to New Trier High School as well. In the photos, we look like old friends. We were in a sea of superstars and I even shook Chaplin's hand.

This was all later reported by *Chicago Sun Times* columnist, Irv Kupcinet, whom I called with the story. He featured it in his column and even said that "[Karger] will be a big man on campus when he returns to the University of Denver."

This was one of the most memorable moments of my life. And it was all the more surreal because security was incredibly tight at the ceremony. Chaplin had received death threats because of his supposed Communist ties of the past. He had been exiled from the U.S. and had lived in Switzerland for many years. This was his triumphant return, and Hollywood was very excited.

There's more to that night. At the party at The Bistro, I'd met Allan Carr, real name Allan Solomon. Originally from Highland Park, the suburb next to Glencoe, he was a personal manager to some pretty big stars. He was famous for turning around careers, and his roster of clients included Tony Curtis, Peter Sellers, and Ann-Margret. He was also famous for discovering talent—Michelle Pfeiffer, Olivia Newton-John, and Mark Hamill, to name a few. At the party, he "discovered" me, and I asked for his help to find celebrities to come to our fundraiser in Denver. (He was our brightest hope. In the end, however, we came up empty.)

Now, at the exclusive Governor's Ball party after the Oscars, he told me he'd seen me on stage. He handed me his card and said, "You have to call me. You should be an actor. You crashed the Oscars. This is incredible. I want to hear about this."

Honestly, until this conversation, I never thought about an acting career. I'd been in a few plays in high school. Maybe one in college. I had no training, had never taken a course, but I had played numerous roles in crashing events over the years.

A few words about the art of crashing—because I think some of the traits necessary to be a good crasher not only helped me as an actor, but also as a political consultant, and now as a candidate. First off, I'm a very determined guy. I don't take no for an answer. On those occasions when I have been thrown out of events—and there have been plenty—I become even more determined to get back in. Second, look like you belong. Dress appropriately (no flowered shirts) and act like you are supposed to be there. Finally, the ability to read people is essential. You have to assess each situation. (I would usually take the nice guy approach.

You don't want to be a jerk. If you get stopped, you just kind of play dumb.)

Even when I have a ticket to an event, I'm still thinking to myself: *how would I get in if I didn't have this ticket?* A recent example: on election night in November 2010, the folks at *Politico* invited me to their exclusive party at the Newseum in Washington, DC. Frankly, it was not nearly as much fun because I was on the list.

I definitely wasn't on the list to get on Hubert Humphrey's campaign plane in early June of 1972. After losing the California presidential primary, the former vice president left the Beverly Hilton Hotel for Houston to address the National Governor's Association. My ex-girlfriend Barb Fine and I talked our way onto his plane and flew overnight to Texas with Humphrey and the press.

***

My parents were not only expecting me to return to Chicago after college and join my father's firm. They were expecting me to settle down and marry a nice girl.

Marriage wasn't for me. Nor was Chicago. It wasn't that I disliked the city or even being around my parents. I simply realized it would be problematic to be a closeted gay man in my hometown. Whenever I had walked around with my boyfriend Dan, I'd been scared to death that I'd run into somebody I knew. How would I explain to a friend of the family what I was doing with another man, whom no one knew?

California appealed to me for a few reasons. First and foremost, it was far away. It was also warm. And it offered an excuse. Tenuous as it was, I could honestly say that I had a great opportunity out there; a big time manager said he could make me a star ... or at least launch an acting career.

My parents and I worked out a compromise. I'd stay in Chicago at least through the winter holidays. Instead of joining my father, I'd work as a full-time volunteer in Senator Percy's re-election campaign. I'd already been doing some work on the Denver campus, registering potential Republican voters from Illinois and arranging for absentee ballots for those who wouldn't be in town to vote. And instead of living with my parents in Glencoe, I'd live in the city.

Thanks to my inheritance from Uncle Buddy, I had enough money to support myself for a while. But my dad offered to pay the rent on a small studio apartment I found on the north side, not too far west of Lake Shore Drive. I'd always had roommates, so this was the first time I'd been on my own, free to lead a gay life—as long as I didn't run into anybody.

My apartment wasn't too far away from Halsted Street. Today, Halsted is in the center of an area that is home to many gay bars. In 1972, there were only a few. As in Denver, there was a handful of darkly-lit drinking establishments. People would either stand outside or go inside and cruise the decidedly seedy environs.

The bar where I'd seen Buddy featured dancing. In many places, however, it was illegal for two men to dance with each other. Police raids weren't all that uncommon. Such laws gave rise to the crudely named phenomenon of the "fag hag." Gay guys would bring a girl along so that the three of them could dance together without fear of getting arrested.

Chuck Percy had little difficulty topping his Democratic challenger, Congressman Roman Pucinski. My guy won 68% of the vote, even more than President Nixon. I've now worked on elections for over forty years. This one was among the easiest.

It was also among the most fun. At age twenty-two, I had quite a bit of responsibility and got to spend a considerable amount of time with an incumbent United States senator. Percy's goddaughter Carolyn Taylor and I organized a three-week bus tour around the state for the senator and his family. Once I picked him up at his mother's house in our Greyhound-sized bus, "The Percy Express."

The election was held November 7. With my parents' blessing, I planned to move to California after the first of the year. When my lease was up on November 15, I moved out of my apartment and headed to Glencoe, where I planned to stay until I headed west.

I arrived home to find my mother sobbing and the Glencoe police waiting to talk to me.

Mr. Karger,

I actually found you tonight by accident and I do believe I am going to be staying up all night reading about you!

I had been mulling over a potential political career for myself; many, many friends and acquaintances have encouraged me to run (State House). I just didn't think it was possible at all for me. I'm a hardcore Republican, which works well, but I'm also gay which I didn't think would. But now as I'm reading your story I'm just getting filled with so much hope that it's possible.

I'm sorry for going on like this! I am just so excited now.

I'd love to have a conversation with you sometime when you're not too terribly busy (a moment which may not come for you anytime soon!).

Thank you again.

J.P.

CHAPTER THREE

"DO YOU MIND IF I BRING ROMAN POLANSKI?"

In early March 1973, I load up my new car for the move to California. It's a red Cougar convertible. I think that's what people drive in Hollywood. I'm not sure, because I don't know a soul out there except for Allan Carr, the talent manager who said he could get me into show business.

Heading out there without a job or place to live or any friends is not so much evidence of chutzpah, but, rather, desperation. The last four months have been excruciatingly difficult. Now, thank heavens, I can finally escape.

I'm still in the driveway when my mother comes out of the house. She gives me a hug and a kiss and then, with tears in her eyes, says, "Promise me one thing."

"What's that?"

"Promise me you won't do X-rated movies."

How bizarre.

Now, if she'd have said, "Please don't get into trouble," that would have made sense.

***

As the midterm elections of 2010 approached, the witty, right-on *New York Times* columnist Gail Collins noted that the body politic was digging deep into the past to sully the reputations of candidates from all parties. She then posed an important question: "Candidates deserve to be able to throw a cloak of invisibility over youthful indiscretion, but what's the limit?"

As someone who spent more than a quarter of a century as a political consultant and often did opposition research, I agree with Ms. Collins' answer: "First of all, nothing anyone did in college short of a felony should count against them."

In the interest of transparency (and aware that opponents might wish to dig up dirt on me), I feel the need to report one significant indiscretion from those college years. In the previous chapter, I detailed my 1972 Academy Awards escapade. As the late, great radio broadcaster Paul Harvey used to say, here's "the *rest* of the story." It's a story of inexcusable personal behavior that still makes me cringe. I financed that trip to L.A. my senior year using a stolen credit card. I didn't need to, but I did anyway.

A few weeks before I even knew I'd be going on that trip, I was in downtown Denver for a meeting. After the meeting ended, political junkie that I was, I decided to stop at the State Capitol and just walk around. It was after hours, so all the offices were closed. A janitor was in the hallway outside the door marked "Office of the Lieutenant Governor."

As I've already said, I was always curious, always liked to push the envelope. I'd love to sneak in offices and see what I could get away with. Senior year in particular, I pushed even harder.

I told the janitor that I had met with the lieutenant governor earlier in the day and had forgotten my briefcase. "Can you let me back in so I can see if it's there?"

I guess I have an honest face. He opened the door and went about his business.

Thrilled to be alone in the office of the second-highest-ranking political figure in the state, I made myself at home in the big chair behind the desk. Then I opened a drawer, looking for a souvenir to commemorate the visit. As I recall I found a placard marked, "Parking Reserved for Lt. Governor" and a notepad with the letterhead, "Office of Lieutenant Governor." I took them and opened another drawer. Inside it were several credit cards, all unsigned. I pocketed one: a Bank Americard (the Visa of its day). Then I left.

When it came time to go to Los Angeles in search of our dance marathon celebrity, I had enough money in my own bank account to pay for the trip. Instead, stupidly, I used the lieutenant governor's Bank Americard. For airline tickets, meals, even our tuxedos. On a couple of occasions, I had to do some fast talking to a quizzical clerk or salesperson, but I returned to school thinking I'd pulled it off.

I didn't use the card again and figured that the lieutenant governor wouldn't get the bill until I'd stopped using it, and Bank Americard wouldn't pursue the culprit. Six months later, as I drove to my parents' house on the eve of my permanent move to California, I certainly wasn't thinking about it.

But the lieutenant governor *had* reported the stolen card. And the Los Angeles Police Department had taken over from there. It's a complicated story of how they finally tracked down Dave and me. Briefly, the tuxedo store clerk had seen us on television during the Academy Awards, and he identified us when he was shown the tape of the closing ceremony. The cops searched through Denver-area school yearbooks, and the clerk identified us from our fraternity photos.

And so in mid-November 1972, the Glencoe police came to my folks' house and told them they had a warrant for my arrest on seven counts of bunco and forgery. I was already en route home (still no cell phones). The officers told my parents that when I arrived, I should come up to the police station and turn myself in.

I entered to find my mother in tears. "Tell me you didn't do this," she sobbed. My dad was all business. He had already called our cousin Frank "Denny" Mayer, Jr., a prominent lawyer. Denny arrived a few minutes after I did—still dressed in black tie, fresh from an engagement he had attended—with a fellow lawyer from his firm with criminal defense experience. We went to the police station and I was served the arrest warrant. (The police promised not to alert the local newspapers, and remarkably, there was never any coverage except for one paragraph in the town weekly, the *Glencoe News*, in which I was misidentified as Fred *Targer*.)

Over the next few months, as I worked as a sales clerk at Saks Fifth Avenue in the local shopping center, some skilled lawyers worked on my behalf in Chicago and Los Angeles. In mid-February 1973, we reached an agreement. Because I made restitution, because I didn't have a previous record, and, let's face it, because I had a "dream team" of lawyers, all the charges were dropped. When the final hearing took place in L.A., the Los Angeles Police Department investigators (who were actually quite impressed by the caper and told us how much fun they had, including interviewing Ann-Margret) asked us to fill in a few missing details. I was given three year's probation and a fine of, I think, $500. Dave received the same deal. Whatever records we had have been expunged by the state.

This shameful episode straightened me out for life. I was doing all kinds of crazy stuff during my college years. Going into offices and taking souvenirs came to a screeching halt. The adrenaline rush was replaced by chronic fear and paranoia. It sounds clichéd, but it was a good thing I got caught. I was a daring kid. I had a little money then and was not in a good place. I felt I had nothing to lose. It seemed more likely I'd end up like Uncle Buddy than like Dan Brewster. The credit card caper was my wake up call.

***

I confess: I didn't give up crashing. The 45th Academy Awards were held on March 27, 1973. Newly arrived in Los Angeles, I was there.

It turned out that every security guard had a photo of me from 1972, and I was even escorted out once. But thanks to that same white badge from the previous year and some fast-talking, I managed to get back in just in time to walk best actress winner Liza Minnelli to the front of the stage for the closing ceremony. I remained on stage behind her and best supporting actor winner Joel Grey (and next to best supporting actress winner Eileen Heckart, James Coburn, and Dyan Cannon) as we all sang "You Oughta Be in Pictures." A photo of the six of us was prominently featured in the *Los Angeles Times* the next day.

The *Hollywood Reporter* even covered my crashing escapades. "One of the late-staying guests at the marvelous Bistro party co-hosted by Marshall Field and Bailey K. Howard was the young, handsome Fred Karger, who admitted to Marshall's bride Jamie Fields [whom my brother used to date in Chicago] that he crashed for the second year in a row. He also crashed the 1972 Oscars and was seen shaking Chaplin's hand."

The paper didn't mention that I also crashed the Governor's Ball again. If Candace Bergen, who accepted an honorary award for her father, ever wonders who the "young, handsome" man with whom she posed at the Ball was, it's me—dressed in a more tasteful tux shirt, which I had purchased with my own money.

During the first Oscars crash, I had learned that it's essential to arrive at the ceremony in a limousine. Dave and I had successfully commandeered an empty limo that had just dropped people off and then paid the chauffeur to drive around the block and deposit us in front. (Then I managed to walk down the red carpet, just after I slipped a note to the MC that I was a star. "Here comes Jerry Mathers of 'Leave It to Beaver,'" announced Army Archerd, the celebrity columnist introducing everyone arriving at the event. At the time there were rumors, untrue, that the Beave had been killed in Vietnam, so there was quite a stir.)

In 1974, my third straight ceremony, the limo not only got me to the front door, it got me backstage. I wasn't sure how I was going to crash that year until—unbelievable as it might seem—I found an all-access badge sitting on the backseat of the limousine my friends and I had flagged down. Bingo. I grabbed it and asked the driver who his previous passenger had been. "John Huston," he said. The legendary director was one of the co-hosts of that night's ceremony.

(I never tried to crash the ceremony after 1974. Years later, however, in 2006, I talked my way into the posh *Vanity Fair* after-party by displaying a phony Oscar I'd bought. I showed it to security and said I'd won it for Visual Effects that night.) I had always wondered if that fake Oscar statue that I bought years earlier would work. It did.

When I crashed the Oscars in '73, I'd only been in L.A. for a few weeks. On arriving, I stayed in a motel in Westwood, not too far from UCLA, while I looked for an apartment. I'd had no idea where to settle, but Pug Schoen, one of my brother's best friends who had gone to USC, had told me right before I left Chicago, "You want to live just west of the 405 Freeway between Wilshire and Santa Monica. West L.A., great location, very affordable."

It was good advice. I rented a furnished one-bedroom apartment. There were a lot of characters living in that building on Wellesley Drive, including a stripper who had moved in because she worked at The Ball, a private strip club a few blocks away on Wilshire Boulevard. I liked the club and promptly joined because it was lots of fun.

My first order of business was to look up Allan Carr. He was producing Ann-Margret's act in Las Vegas, so we arranged to meet over there in the showroom at Caesar's Palace during her rehearsal. I had told him about the credit card caper, and he was so fascinated that he said he wanted to make a movie about it.

A little later, Ann-Margret wandered down from the stage. "This is the guy that took the credit card that they interviewed you about," Allan told her. The detectives had secured the film of me on stage with her at the Oscars and had asked her if she remembered who I was. In her sex kitten voice, now Ann-Margret purred to me,

"Oh, yeah, whatever happened to those guys?" Apparently, she didn't get the point. I was one of those guys.

Back in L.A., Allan had me come to his office at 9000 Sunset Boulevard. There he advised me where to go to acting school. He also told me I needed photos for a composite, recommended a photographer, and suggested we shoot at his mansion. I was pretty certain he was attracted to me, but I never let on that I was gay. And he never made a move.

Allan also invited me to parties at his Benedict Canyon home. This was heaven for a star-struck 23-year-old who dreamed of hanging out with Dino Martin and Desi Arnaz, Jr. Never did, but I'd mix poolside with Judy Garland's actress-daughter Lorna Luft and other young stars of the time.

Allan was Hollywood's most famous party-thrower during the seventies. The stars, producers, directors, and casting agents turned out for these bashes in abundance. I was always on the guest list, too.

One of the best parties was thrown for Mick Jagger and the Rolling Stones after their L.A. concert. It was called "from midnight 'til dawn," and the recommended dress was "glitter." I rode up the long driveway in a shuttle bus with the Village People and thought that I was really underdressed. Lots of stars were there, including some old favorites like Tony Curtis and Rosalind Russell.

The headshots of me taken by Allan's guy cost a fortune and turned out to be a bust because they were all too dark. Fortunately the next photographer I went to, a kind of scruffy, but talented guy named Buddy Rosenberg, came through. I added his best shots to a resume that I was advised to embellish. Some of those college skits turned into outright plays!

Although I was also advised to mail photos and resume to agents who represented talent for commercials, I decided to hand-deliver them. *Who knows*, I thought, *maybe I'll be able to talk my way in to see an agent.* I had the time.

As luck would have it, I was at the reception desk of the Jack Wormser Agency when a woman came out from the office area. I approached her. Her name was Sandy Joseph and she happened to be from Chicago. She was on her way to the bathroom, but I gave her my packet. "Wait here. I want to talk to you," she said. A few minutes later we went to her office and she ended up signing me.

Wormser, now called KSR, was one of the top commercial agencies in town. Its client roster included several big name actors. Soon I was auditioning for commercials. And soon I had my first job—a spot for Straw Hat Pizza Palace in which I rode a bicycle along with two other actors to promote a contest. Not only did I make some money; more importantly, I could now join the Screen Actors Guild (SAG).

The guild was very hard to get into. In Hollywood then and now, for all intents and purposes, you can't work in television, film, or commercials unless you are a member of SAG. And you can't become a member unless you work in one of those fields. It's a tricky Catch-22. But thanks to Sandy Joseph, I was now set and could audition for other commercials and television roles.

At the same time I was auditioning for commercials, I was receiving my first formal training at the Lee Strasberg Institute.

Despite Allan's recommendation, I wasn't impressed by the program at Strasberg. Besides, it was more geared for theater, not film, and I had moved to Hollywood to get a television series, not act in plays.

After going to classes for a few months at Strasberg, I found out that the hottest acting workshop in town was run by Charles Conrad, who had studied with the legendary Sanford Meisner in New York. Although enrollment was very selective, I did well enough in my audition to be admitted to a beginners class. My fellow actors there included Les Moonves (now head of CBS), Suzanne Sommers, my longtime scene partner Lynda Carter, and a host of great looking men and beautiful women. Many were very well-connected in the business.

I made a lot of good friends there. We tried to help each other out professionally and we had a lot of parties. When I moved from the Wellesley Drive apartment to a nicer one-bedroom apartment in Beverly Hills, I loved to entertain. Before one of my parties, one of the really cute girls in my class, named Honey, called and asked, "Do you mind if I bring Roman Polanski?" This was the post-"Chinatown," pre-rape-charges Polanski. Did I mind? Are you kidding?

Parties are a great networking tool in Hollywood. I barely spoke to Polanski and he never offered me a role, but I met some people at Allan Carr's house who proved to be extremely helpful. Producer Jon Epstein and director Jim Sheldon were veterans with long lists of television credits. They were part of a kind of "gay Mafia" that looked out for the brotherhood. Taking me under their wings, they pointed me to a dialect coach and even a ballet class to loosen my movement. Just as my brother had gotten his MBA from

52

Northwestern's business school, this was my graduate school training, and I took it very seriously.

Jon and Jim also helped get me my first television role. On an episode of ABC's popular "Owen Marshall, Counselor at Law," I played Deke Palmer, a clean-cut, wealthy college student who was dealing drugs. During a deal gone bad, I killed a policeman. His partner (played by Tim Matheson, who would go on to starring roles in "Animal House" and numerous TV series such as "The West Wing") stalked me and then shot me in self-defense as I tried to run him over with my sports car.

Titled "Killer with a Badge," the episode aired in February 1974. In addition to Matheson, it featured some real pros like regulars Arthur Hill and Lee Majors (in his last episode before leaving to star in his own series, "Six Million Dollar Man") and Richard Anderson, who starred as my father. Emmy-winning actor Scott Jacoby played my younger brother, and Nicholas Hammond, who had played Frederick in "The Sound of Music," played my drug dealer.

I was my own publicist, and notified the Chicago-area press when the show would appear. This was before the age of VHS and Beta, much less Tivo and DVR. Fortunately, Leonard Grant, a friend who was a personal manager, had one of the first VCRs, a ¾-inch videotape cassette machine. These early models were so expensive that few people outside show business bought them. Another drawback: the tape was only twenty minutes long. Luckily, I was killed nineteen minutes into the show. So if you're interested, you can go to YouTube to see me in my first role on television. (http://www.youtube.com/watch?v=Kk5fhI3P-gQ)

Watching this, my first performance, I'd give myself a C minus. At twenty-three, I was still a long way from mastering the craft. My movements were a bit wooden and my delivery of lines was pretty flat.

I think I improved in later roles, including two episodes of "McMillan and Wife," starring Rock Hudson and Susan Saint James. I played a policeman in one and a doctor in another. Still, you'll never hear me say I was a great actor. I was always too nervous about memorizing and delivering my lines to lose myself in a character.

This was true at auditions, too. The pressure was tremendous, and I lost a lot of roles that I was right for due to nerves. Jon was the producer of the TV series, "Rich Man, Poor Man," based on his successful mini-series. This version was set when the brothers were younger. I had a great shot at the Peter Strauss role, which eventually went to James Carroll Jordan, but my audition did not go well. I ended up with a small part in the mini-series, only playing the editor of the college newspaper. (You know it's a small role when you don't have a name.)

I might still be in the business if I hadn't blown another tryout. This one was in front of producer/writer Steven Bochco. Before he created such series hits as "Doogie Howser, M.D.," "Hill Street Blues," "L.A. Law," and "NYPD Blue," there was "Richie Brockelman, Private Eye."

Richie was a young Jewish college student who worked his way through school as a private detective. There couldn't have been a more perfect role for me. Bochco agreed. He basically told me that the role was mine if I was up to it.

Nope. Too much pressure. I was so nervous, I bombed the audition.

Bochco was not gay, but I often socialized with gay agents and producers and directors like George Cukor (who directed such movies as "The Philadelphia Story" and "My Fair Lady"), Frank McCarthy (who directed "Patton"), and Ross Hunter (producer of "Pillow Talk" and many other successful Rock Hudson and Doris Day movies for Universal as well as "Airport") and William Frye ("Airport '75," in which I had a small role). Virtually all of these men were closeted. When they went to parties or award shows, they were almost always accompanied by their lovers and often two other women (then called "beards"), ostensibly their dates.

Ross Hunter and his longtime partner, a wonderful man named Jacques Mapes, were together for some forty years. Jon Epstein and I went to several dinner parties at their grand house in Trousdale Estates. Everyone in Hollywood knew these men were gay. Yet they rarely went out as a couple. Instead, you'd read that Ross Hunter and Nancy Sinatra and Jacque Mapes and Loretta Young were seen dining at such-and-such a restaurant.

The Hollywood press wasn't fooled; they just saw no reason to expose this. Certainly gay people are accepted more today than they were thirty-five years ago. But at the same time, today's 24/7 cable shows, gossip magazines, and the blogosphere are much more interested in outing people than the press was when I was trying to make it as an actor. One thing that sadly hasn't changed: now, as then, being an openly gay actor is most likely a career-killer.

Jon was also very good friends with Rock Hudson. Rock and Tom Clark were together for fifteen years and lived in a beautiful home off Coldwater Canyon in Beverly Hills. The four of us would have dinner prepared by their cook, and then they'd screen a movie in their home theatre, complete with a projectionist courtesy of Universal Studios. In November 1975, I went to Rock's fiftieth birthday party, a star-studded costume affair. I came as a priest.

Rock was a real gentleman, somewhat shy. He always remembered me because I had the same name as a famous composer and musician, Freddie Karger. He came to my house once, when I threw a birthday party for Jon. By that time he had broken up with Tom and was dating Mark Christian, the young man who would end up suing the Hudson estate alleging that Rock had exposed him to AIDS. Tom returned when Rock became ill.

Socializing wasn't always limited to house parties. There were several gay bars and clubs in Los Angeles. I was at the black tie 1974 opening of Scott Forbes' Studio One, a West Hollywood night club and discotheque located in a huge old factory building. As Forbes, an optometrist and community activist, told the *Los Angeles Times*: "Studio One was designed, planned, and conceived for gay people, gay male people." The club had strobe lights, a hall of mirrors, and a dance floor that could and did accommodate over one thousand people.

In their book, *Gay L.A.: A History of Sexual Outlaws, Power Politics, and Lipstick Lesbians*, authors Lillian Faderman and Stuart Timmons write: "Studio One was widely regarded as the number one dance spot, straight or gay. Music promoters vied to have their records played there....It was dubbed by many newspapers and magazines as one of the most exciting discos in the country."

Agreed. It was even more exciting because in the rear of the building sat the Back Lot Theater. Here, booked by Leonard Grant, big name acts like Joan Rivers and Wayland Flowers and Madame performed.

For a gay man like me, Studio One was nirvana—great music, great looking patrons (gay and straight, but mostly gay), and great looking bartenders (uniformly gay, I believe). Most important, out on the dance floor or at the bar, I was free to be myself, live my life honestly, act on my gayness. For the first time in my life, I felt popular. I spent most of my twenties there and met many of my friends and boyfriends on that dance floor.

Sadly, for gay celebrities like Rock Hudson, Studio One was simply too public. Rock and others in the business fearful of being outed found it safer to go an hour down the 405 to Laguna Beach and its main bar, called the Boom Boom Room. (Later in the book, you'll see how, in a sense, this bar is responsible for my current political endeavors.)

You'd think that having found a safe haven to be gay, I would have stopped dating women and even trying to sleep with them. But you'd be wrong. In part to keep the charade going for my acting career as well as with family and friends, I kept at it.

I went out with Miss California-World, Brenda Dickson, a star of "The Young and the Restless" whom I met at a Jon Epstein party. A photo of me feeding her shrimp appeared in a soap opera magazine. Had the caption identified us as a couple, I'd have banked a lot of capital in covering up my gayness. Instead, it read:

"Brenda Dickson may look like she's having fun with young actor Fred Karger, but she's really pining after her boyfriend in London...." A few years later I dated another star from "The Young and the Restless," Terry Lester, the handsome blond male lead on the show. Bet not too many people can say they dated both leads.

Terry and I and the other men I dated were careful where we went. As a result, two time zones away from home, I remained confident that my double life was still a secret. Then a friend spoke out of turn to another friend.

Mr. Karger—

Thank you for your reply. It brought tears to my eyes to read your campaign promise from none other than a fellow gay man. My mate and I were outed by his parents while I was at their place for the semester break. Worse than them throwing me away like rotting trash for simply being in a loving committed relationship with their son, the closest person to my heart, they crushed him, mind, body, and soul that night. People I once trusted called me the most vile of things, and cast me out.

It is such a cruel fate being born who we are. I ask myself if there are gods why would they be so cruel to allow such evil against innocence to happen. I vow as a psychologist to end this damn debate on our lives once and for all even if it costs me my own. I see so much suffering of our people, especially our youth, every day doing what I do and it's becoming unbearable. I just want it to end and that hope, that it will, was renewed when I found your page....

They say never give up hope, but... I was getting close. Thank you for restoring it. I just hope that my work and my fight for equality alongside people like you will get us there before the end of our lives. Take care, Mr. Karger, right now you are my hero.

C.

CHAPTER FOUR

"THERE'S SOMETHING I HAVE TO ASK YOU."

Late December 1975. My longtime close friend and fellow Denver University graduate Gary Wolfson has come to pick me up at my parents' house. When I come home from California for Christmas every year, I always put together a group dinner of three or four close friends and their wives or dates.

Gary does what he always does when he comes over—what we used to do surreptitiously when we were teenagers—heads to my father's liquor cabinet. He fixes himself a particularly large Scotch. Then he looks over his shoulder to see if we're alone and says, "There's something I have to ask you."

Gary tells me that over the last few months, he has heard rumors from two different college classmates. One of them, Jill Rubin, lives in Sun Valley. She owned, and still does, Irv's Red Hots—the famous Chicago hot dog stand named for her father. Apparently she met a friend of mine from Hollywood who was skiing up there—it was director Jim Sheldon—who let it slip that I was gay. She refused to believe it—shows what a good actor I was at least on that front—but she asked a few friends like Gary, who also dismissed the assertion and got upset with her for even suggesting it.

Gary kept the rumor to himself. But another alum, Greg Kravett, didn't. He called Gary and several other friends.

I've been dreading and looking forward to this moment for years. It's been so hard to keep this secret from my close friends. It almost seems like I've betrayed them. Yet, as close as they are I can't be certain how they'll react ... and if they'll play along with the charade so that my parents don't find out. When it comes to Ward and June, I'm filled only with dread.

"Yes, it's true," I say. We have a long talk.

Gary is wonderful. No recriminations. He tells me that he's been dating a girl whose sister is a lesbian and that lately he's hung out with a lot of gay people. "It makes absolutely no difference," he says. He tells me that he didn't suspect I was gay, but he had thought I'd been hiding something because I often disappeared for weekends or several days at a time.

Moved by Gary's acceptance, I soon have "the talk" and come out to three other close friends from Glencoe and DU, Rob Weinstein, Bill Solomon, and Jerry Blumberg. They respond just as positively.

Remarkably, these four and the small circle of other friends from home whom I soon tell will keep my secret to themselves. It will be another fifteen years before I share the news with my unsuspecting parents and brother.

***

The scene with Gary went more smoothly than a scene I'd had a few months earlier on the television show, "Ellery Queen." I had only four short lines, but they were important because one was the cue for about half a dozen characters to enter. Simple. Yet every time I tried to deliver them, I froze—either misspoke or couldn't get the words out at all.

Jim Sheldon was directing. He was wonderfully patient. So were the actors, including Betty White, Bert Parks, Jim Hutton, David Wayne, and Eve Arden, whom I'd grown up loving on the series, "Our Miss Brooks."

"Just relax, honey, it's okay," Miss Arden said.

Six takes. It was so embarrassing. Such moments were happening all too often on sets and at auditions. Maybe it was time to get out of the business.

Sensing that I was floundering, my acting coach Charles Conrad came to my rescue. He was a kind, brilliant, high-energy guy, and such a fine teacher that I had progressed to his advanced class. One day, as I completed a scene in front of several classmates, he blurted out, "You need to go to est, Fred."

I had never heard of est, which stands for Erhard Seminar Training. Started in California in the early 1970s by former publishing executive Werner Erhard, est was one of the early entrants in the human potential movement. "We want nothing short of a total transformation—an alteration of substance, not a change of form," said Erhard, who had changed his name from John Paul Rosenberg. "Life is always perfect just the way it is. When you realize that, then no matter how strongly it may appear to be otherwise, you know that whatever is happening right now will turn out all right. Knowing this, you are in a position to begin mastering life."

est consisted of two intense weekend seminars in which you weren't allowed to get up to go to the bathroom or attend to other needs. I then went to several follow-up seminars. It was life-altering.

There were 250 people in these classes, and they told the worst stories in the world. I heard terrible tales of incest, abuse, you name it. I still remember how moved we all were when a cute young girl shared that she had been stung by a bee once and nearly died. The doctor had told her that if it ever happened again, she would die. She lived in fear every day.

I talked about the trauma of Uncle Buddy's death, but didn't reveal that I was gay. I wasn't ready to do that to 250 strangers. But I will say that after hearing all the tales of woe, I concluded that dealing with being gay or having low self-esteem seemed like a small problem compared to what others faced.

For me, mastering life meant finding a different calling than acting. I had given myself two to three years to make it. Now it was time to move on. What was my true love? Politics. est accelerated the transition.

I'd flirted with finding a job in politics during the California gubernatorial race of 1974 in which Democrat Jerry Brown won his first term, beating my candidate, Republican Houston Flournoy. I even went into Flournoy headquarters for an interview, but after only one year in town at that point, I felt I hadn't given acting a fair chance. My dad was covering the expense of my acting classes, so the wolf was not at my door.

Now, two years later I did more than flirt. While continuing to go on auditions and to acting classes, I volunteered full time for Robert Finch, who was running in the 1976 Republican primary for the U.S. Senate. The campaign was being run by Bill Roberts, a well-known political consultant, who with the equally well-known Stu Spencer had managed Ronald Reagan's campaigns for governor. Spencer was now managing President Ford's campaign.

The moderate Finch had been elected lieutenant governor of California in 1966, garnering more votes than his running mate, one Governor Ronald Reagan. In 1969, he had moved on to serve as President Nixon's first secretary of Health, Education and Welfare. Now, his primary opponent for the Senate was the outspoken conservative president of San Francisco State University, S.I. Hayakawa.

Along with another full time volunteer, Bill Naeve, I was in charge of youth outreach. We sent the candidate and other speakers to colleges around the state.

A few weeks before the election, the campaign ran out of money. Naeve and I were instructed to start calling those who had already given and to ask for more. Our quarry was the low paying donor—$100 or less. We were considered too young and green to solicit the heavy hitters. But as we hit pay dirt, persuading $100 donors to up the ante to $250, we were given the green light to call $1000 donors. That was the maximum then, but spouses who hadn't given were fair game. Successful at this level, too, we became the young stars of the office.

Finch lost the primary, but I won the respect of one of the fundraising heads, Audrey Boyle. She soon offered me my first paid political job as finance director for Ralph Andrews, a Republican running for the state assembly. Andrews (not to be confused with Ralph Edwards) was the producer of several television game shows, including "You Don't Say" and "Liars Club." He was a real character, shaving his head years before it became fashionable and driving around town in a gold Rolls Royce.

Living in a predominantly Democratic district, Andrews lost, too. And he lost again four months later in a special election for the California State Senate. I was deputy campaign manager for that effort, working for another political pro, Allan Hoffenblum.

The presidential campaign of 1976 was among the most exciting in history, as Reagan challenged the sitting president Gerald Ford for the Republican nomination. As a zealous, moderate Young Republican, I was firmly in Ford's camp (earning me some enemies for life in California). I first worked for him at the convention in Kansas City.

My beat—thanks to a call from Roberts to Spencer—was a hotel room organized and led by Ford's chief delegate hunter, the future White House chief of staff and secretary of state, Jim Baker. I reported directly to him. One of my duties—along with Bill Naeve—was to escort delegates to meetings with President Ford.

To clinch the nomination, Ford needed to persuade the Mississippi delegation to drop a winner-takes-all rule and let each delegate vote individually. I took them to several meetings in the president's suite. Unfortunately, they would often show up late, causing me great anxiety.

Shortly before a crucial procedural vote that would in all likelihood determine the nominee, I was lucky enough to be one of the first to know that Mississippi was going to drop the winner-takes-all rule. After their face-to-face, the president and the Mississippians were all smiles. The delegates exited carrying all kinds of campaign hats, pens, badges, you name it. What an exciting time that was for a 26-year-old.

In what turned out to be the last contested Republican convention, Ford eked out the win. Then in a show of unity, Reagan nominated him. The speech was so powerful that I, like many others, stood on the convention floor and wondered if we had nominated the wrong man. Ford was a great guy and he stabilized the country after the Watergate debacle and Nixon's resignation, but Reagan had such charisma. As a budding political consultant, I could see that he had all the attributes necessary for success at the ballot box and in the Oval Office. He lit up the Kansas City convention hall and the nation. His optimism and strong convictions were riveting. The divide between the conservative wing of the party and me was narrowing thanks to Ronald Reagan.

***

A funny thing happened on my way to the political arena. I enjoyed my greatest success as an actor. Knowing that I was getting out of the business, realizing that a muffed audition wasn't the end of the world, I loosened up and became pretty good at my craft.

During the summer of 1976, I had another scrape with a credit card—literally. This one, however, was as positive as can be. Here's what happened:

In a bar in the valley, I ran into Len Cutler, a Leo Burnett advertising executive whom I had dated in Chicago. He was in town to shoot a commercial for Edge Shaving Cream. At the bar he suddenly said, "Oh my God, Fred, you'd be perfect for it."

My eyes lit up.

"Have your agent call first thing Monday morning."

At 9:01 a.m., I was on the phone with my agent. "Oh, we submitted you for that and they turned you down," she said.

"Well, resubmit me. I have a very good contact." This was a big deal. National commercials pay big bucks.

After the first audition, I was called back two or three more times. And then ... I got the job! One of my two major goals when I moved to California had been realized: a major national commercial. Besides knowing I was in for a nice payday, I was excited because I'd beaten out one of my friends from acting school, Bryan Montgomery, who had done dozens of national commercials.

My success had less to do about acting and more to do about my beard pattern. In the commercial, I face the camera head on. Dressed in a white undershirt, I hold a microphone under my chin. The announcer takes a credit card and swipes it on both sides of my unshaven face. It sounds the same on each.

Then Edge is applied to one side of my face, while "the leading foam" is applied to the other. I shave. "Thirty minutes later" the announcer again applies the credit card. The noise from the non-Edge side is clearly louder, obviously because the shave wasn't as close and some stubble remains. Q.E.D. that, "Edge lets you shave closer than the leading foam."

The late director John Hughes, like me then, just an unknown 26-year-old from suburban Chicago, was hired by Leo Burnett to write and shoot the commercial. It doesn't have the twists and turns of "Home Alone," "Ferris Bueller's Day Off," and so many more wonderful movies he'd go on to direct, but it has become a classic. I can't tell you the number of people I've met who are familiar with the thirty-second spot, including some who weren't even born when it first appeared.

Commercials in those days ran in thirteen-week cycles. To my delight, this one ran for three years! The residuals rolled in, more money than I'd ever made. Thanks in large part to the serendipity of running into Len at that bar, I was able to purchase my house in Laurel Canyon high atop the Hollywood Hills when I was just twenty-seven years old.

At one point Burnett was going to shoot a new version of the commercial, this time with the recognizable face of actor Chuck Connors. If someone had to replace me, I was glad it was Connors. He was one of my heroes, well, *crushes* from childhood. A tall, handsome former major league baseball player, he had starred as Lucas McCain on the popular TV series, "The Rifleman," from 1958 to 1963. As I recall, every three or four episodes, there was some excuse for him to take his shirt off. That was fine with me. I was infatuated. I should have known then and there I was gay!

Connors' mug may have been more recognizable than mine, but it wasn't ready for its Edge close-up. The credit card didn't make the necessary sound when swiped across his face. And so I was granted a reprieve that lasted several more months. Only after another agency, N. W. Ayer, gained the Edge account and launched a different campaign did my spot go off the air.

A final note about this commercial: About five years ago, my cousin Dave Karger, a senior writer at *Entertainment Weekly*,

called to tell me he had seen a feature on John Hughes on the E
Network. "I just saw your commercial!" he said. Then when
Hughes passed away in 2009, CBS opened his obituary on the
national nightly news by showing the spot. Crazy.

My next audition should have prematurely aged my Edge-
smooth face. The stakes were enormous. But, knowing (or at least,
thinking) I would soon be leaving the business, I was remarkably
calm. The show? "Horshack," a highly anticipated spinoff from the
highly successful "Welcome Back, Kotter."

The role? Howard Horshack, cousin of the "Kotter"
regular, Arnold Horshack. But where Arnold was nerdy and
annoying, Howard was hip, if a little bullying. He lived above his
father's costume shop and the schtick was that the father always
made him try on costumes, including ladies wear. *Laugh track,
please.* Howard wasn't quite as cool as Henry Winkler's Fonz from
"Happy Days" or John Travolta's Vinnie Barbarino on "Kotter," but
he was clearly the ladies' man of the show.

The producer? James Komack, the brains behind "Kotter"
and such hits as "Chico and the Man" and "The Courtship of
Eddie's Father." His projects almost always were green-lighted.

At the auditions (there were a few), Ron Palillo (Arnold)
and I just clicked. Because I knew all of the lines and didn't worry
about flubs, I could be spontaneous, get out of myself and act. It
was a lot of fun, and Komack was great.

Knowing I'd done well, I actually wasn't that surprised
when I got the role. The producers signed me to a seven-year
contract with ABC. The state assembly race I'd been working on

was ending. This was my ticket to stardom. Politics would have to wait.

Maybe I jinxed it by telling everybody I had a series. Maybe it was because the script was rewritten every day. Maybe it was because I was destined to enter the political arena and then consider running for president thirty-three years later! Whatever the reason, the show never materialized. A "Kotter" episode in which my TV father and I ended up on the cutting room floor due to time constraints served as the pilot. It bombed and the green light suddenly turned red.

In one of my scenes that was eliminated, my father had me try on a huge hoop skirt from the costume store. I was supposed to look like a Southern belle. This was the only time in my life I was ever in drag. Really. On the day we were rehearsing with the cast of "Kotter," I was introduced to John Travolta while I was wearing a dress. Very embarrassing.

***

If I couldn't be Horshack's cousin, I could be somebody's big brother ... maybe. Some Neanderthals may not believe that gay people have the same parenting desires and instincts as straight folks, but we do. As I hit my mid-twenties, many of my friends were getting married and having kids. So, too, my brother, Dick.

I envied them. I desperately wanted children, but I wasn't going to marry a woman just to become a father; that wasn't for me. Enter the Big Brothers. If I couldn't have a son or daughter, maybe I could have a little brother to play catch with and take to sporting events and just parent a little bit.

I went to the Big Brothers of Greater Los Angeles (BBGLA) office and picked up an application. Then I did some **very** serious thinking. The organization emphasizes that becoming a big brother or sister requires a long commitment; you don't just do it for a few months and change your mind. Yes, I decided, this was something I really wanted to do.

BBGLA is, understandably, extremely cautious in screening its surrogates. The last thing in the world the organization wants to do is expose a child to danger. The application in the mid-1970s asked several background questions, including whether I was a homosexual. I knew that if I answered truthfully I would be categorically denied the opportunity to make a difference in a young person's life and my own. I also knew that my sexual orientation would make no difference in how good or bad I was as a big brother. And I was absolutely certain that I posed no harm to anyone. So I lied.

For the next seven years or so, I was the big brother to a great young man named Tom Ward. He was nine when I was matched with him. His parents were divorced and he lived with his mother and older brother.

We spent at least one day a week together. Tom was not real athletic, but we'd go to the park near his house and throw a baseball or football around. We'd go on hikes, to hockey games, to Dodger games. I'd help him with homework. We participated in a lot of the organized group activities sponsored by BBGLA. I brought him birthday and Christmas presents. When my parents came to visit, we would all get together. It was the only time in my life I really seemed to have a family of my own.

For a while Tom had behavioral problems in school, so I went with his mom Judy to a lot of parent conferences. Sometimes I felt like how I imagined a divorced parent without custody must feel. You don't want to spend your limited amount of time with a youngster being a disciplinarian. I realized, however, that I had to be a good influence on Tom. If he threw trash on the ground, it was my role to tell him to pick it up—whether or not he liked me for doing so.

When a young man reaches sixteen, the program officially ends. During my years with Tom, I became immersed in his family's life, growing close to his mom. After divorcing, she had brought her two sons out to California from Illinois to start a new life. Once settled, she'd become the first woman hired by the California Department of Transportation (CALTRANS) that takes care of landscaping the state's freeways. I respected her. She was lots of fun, too, so at times we'd go out and even go to political events together.

Did I reveal my secret to her? No. Yes, she liked me. Yes, she appreciated what I was doing for Tom. But I had no idea how she would react to the news that the twenty-something young man who had sought out the opportunity to be a big brother to her son was gay.

Speaking of mothers in the dark about my orientation, my mother, the lifelong volunteer, was proud of my involvement with BBGLA. While they obviously would have preferred that I was married with children, my parents were gracious surrogate grandparents. In time, they joined me in annually donating to BBGLA a pair of Dodgers' season tickets that could be used by different big and little brothers and sisters.

73

Over the years, I became more involved with BBGLA, helping plan the Father's Day picnic or getting donations for events. Eventually I was honored to be invited to join the board of directors, which included Roy Disney and many other Los Angeles civic leaders.

I had several gay friends who were also big brothers and who, like me, had to lie on their applications. Today, thank goodness, that is no longer necessary. In opening its doors to gays and lesbians, Big Brothers Big Sisters has been much more tolerant than, for example, the scouting movement. The organization has come to realize that gay big brothers, like gay dads, do not pose a threat because of their orientation. In fact, we may be better parents because it takes such an effort and commitment to have children.

Tom did eventually learn my secret. Shortly after my years with him, he graduated from high school and enlisted in the Army and was stationed in Korea. We lost touch for a while. Then we reconnected, and I sent a Christmas gift for a few years until we lost touch again.

In 2006, his wife Kristen found me on Facebook. This was during the period when I had begun to get publicly involved in gay causes. When Tom learned I was gay, he said something to the effect of, "Yeah, this is cool. I'm glad you can be honest."

Tom and Kristen have three kids and live up in Oregon, where Tom is a paramedic. What do you know? A military-veteran-turned-paramedic has no trouble with a gay man.

***

Not too long after I became Tom's big brother, I went after another role. There was a special election in 1977 for the state assembly in my district. The Democrat was sure to win, so no Republicans were interested in running. At twenty-seven, I felt I had nothing to lose. I felt secure my sexual orientation would not be revealed; I thought I was safely in the closet. I told the party brass that if no one else wanted to run, I would so we'd at least have a name on the ballot. At the last minute, a lawyer named Dana Reed asked me to drop out so that he could run. That was the quickest decision I ever made. "It's all yours," I said. (Dana, who figures in my story years later, lost in a fairly close contest.)

I was the winner. One of the most brilliant people in the history of political consulting hired me to work on Dana's campaign. Two years later, I was jetting around the country with John Connally, a leading contender for the presidency. And this time—as opposed to my flight with Hubert Humphrey—I was actually working for the presidential candidate.

My english is not so good, but I want to congratulate you for your efforts regarding equal rights. Unfortunately I can't vote. If I could, I wouldn't doubt for any second in voting for you. I told to all my American friends about you and everyone is excited.

I hope 2012 will be your year and since I'm from a gay marriage legalized country, Spain, I wish the same for the USA. I'm living here with my boyfriend (we met 2008 in Spain) and due to DOMA (Defense of Marriage Act) it's really complicated to live together.

I know there are a lot of gay people in the same situation and finally everyone gets married with a girlfriend, which is a total lie and a fraud actually, but current US laws make you (as a gay) act like that, because the only thing you care about is being with your boyfriend. Appealing DOMA is the first step for a more equal and a more legal country.

Once again I wish you the best!

Kindly,

Mitchel

CHAPTER FIVE

"HOMOSEXUALITY IS NOT A CONTAGIOUS DISEASE."

November 7, 1978. It is election night, and I am fixated on two races in California for very different reasons. In the first race, Republican George Deukmejian is seeking to become the state's attorney general. As a young member of the Dolphin Group, a political consulting firm, I have served as "Duke's" deputy campaign director. I believe in him and have worked long and hard on his election for the past sixteen months. His victory would be good for the Dolphin Group and for me.

The second race is just as important, but for personal, not professional, reasons. Proposition 6, known as the Briggs' Initiative, is also on the ballot. This ballot initiative seeks to ban gays and lesbians from working in the state's public schools. As a closeted member of the Dolphin Group, I have not been able to campaign openly to defeat Prop 6. But I have worked behind the scenes against this heinous measure, coming as close as I ever have to revealing my secret.

***

My decision to step aside to let Dana Reed run for the state assembly in 1977 did not signal the end of my involvement in that race. By coincidence, Dana hired Bill Roberts as his campaign manager. Bill, in turn, hired me.

A tall, heavy man in his early fifties, Bill was an original, a visionary, a genius, and a mensch. The *New York Times* hailed him as "a founder of political consulting." Street-smart and well-read, he was a news junkie, political junkie, and live-life-to-the-fullest junkie. He was a gambler (frequenting Vegas and L.A.'s legal poker clubs) and a gourmand—not necessarily the best traits to have when you are diabetic—but as he said so often, "I'm not gonna stop livin,' to keep livin.'"

One more thing about Bill: he was generous to a fault. Success never went to his head ... or his clothes. He wore blue leisure suits long after they had gone out of fashion—a phenomenon that did not escape the eye or tongue of Mrs. John Connally when we helped manage her husband's presidential bid in 1980. "Where the devil did you get that suit, Bill?" she asked as we boarded a fancy private jet.

Bill took the question and some teasing in stride. He didn't care. He'd rather give his money away to his family (he never married), friends, or causes. Any time there was a story about a police officer who had been killed or someone trying to raise money for a new kidney or something else, he'd write a check on the spot and send it off. If he could remain anonymous, he did.

Bill had begun his career as an organizer for the Los Angeles County Republican Party. Then in 1960, he and Stu Spencer opened up a consulting firm. Until then, as the *New York Times* also noted, "Political campaigns were virtually always run by amateurs who took time from other work to help out."

Spencer-Roberts & Associates made its first big splash four years later running the campaign of presidential hopeful Nelson Rockefeller in the California primary (the same campaign that I worked on as a 14-year-old in Illinois). In 1966, Stu and Bill managed Ronald Reagan's victorious run for governor of California, and in 1970 they ran his successful bid for reelection. Then in 1974, they parted company.

On his own now, Bill created a new, non-political enterprise. Originally, the Dolphin Group was an investment firm. It also started a for-profit hospice. Soon, however, Bill was itching to be back in the political arena.

In 1976, Stu scratched that itch when he was running President Ford's primary campaign against his old client Ronald Reagan. Ford was in trouble in Florida. Would Bill help?

Bill relocated to the Sunshine State. Ford overcame Reagan's lead down there, won the primary, and the nomination. Bill was back in the saddle. After the 1976 elections, the Dolphin Group focused solely on consulting—for candidates, corporations, associations, and not-for-profits.

As noted earlier, I first met Bill when he was hired at the eleventh hour to try and rescue Bob Finch's 1976 Senate bid. He liked me enough to offer me a job at the Dolphin Group that summer working on behalf of farmers fighting a ballot initiative to write California's Agricultural Labor Relations Act into the state Constitution—Proposition 14. Already committed to helping Ralph Andrews run for state assembly, I had turned down that offer. Now, however, I was available to help in Dana Reed's bid. I hired on for a three-month stint for this special election ... and stayed for the next twenty-seven years.

The Dolphin Group circa 1977 was a bare bones operation. Salaried at $1000 per month, I became the fourth member, joining Bill, fellow consultant Lee Stitzenberger, and advertising director

Jim Rosner, who had been with Spencer-Roberts. Here's a little known fact: political consultants are lucky to break even managing campaigns; they make their money doing the advertising for their candidate-clients.

We had a small rundown office on the second floor of a converted medical building in Westwood—hardly glamorous for a guy who consulted on several presidential campaigns. We all had our own offices. There was also a big open room for campaigns to work out of—what we affectionately called "the bullpen." As we grew we added a receptionist and a bookkeeper. Initially, however, there was no support staff. Lee—another newcomer who would become a lifelong friend—and I took turns answering the phones and doing the bookkeeping.

Political consulting is a cyclical business. When there's an election, you're busy. When there's not an election, an off year, you may not have a single client. During those lean times, Lee and I could be found playing Asteroids, Pole Position, and various video baseball games at an arcade just half a block from our office.

My big break came in the summer of 1977 when Deukmejian retained the Dolphin Group to run his campaign for California attorney general. He contacted us right after Dana's campaign was over. Duke was a 49-year-old Armenian-American lawyer from Long Beach. He had first been elected to the state assembly in 1962 and had become Senate majority leader in 1969. The following year he had finished fourth in the Republican primary for attorney general. Now he was trying again. Few knew his name, and those that did couldn't pronounce it.

Bill managed the effort and gave me the title deputy campaign director. I served as press secretary, too. At just twenty-seven, I was thrown into the water to sink or swim with day-to-day duties on the ground for a statewide campaign in California. Many mornings I'd drive to Long Beach and pick up the candidate and take him to events up and down the state, many of which I had arranged.

George was a devoted family man. He was not that interested in social issues, but had a reputation as a tough law and order guy. He had authored California's "Use a Gun, Go to Prison" law and the state's death penalty statute. Unfortunately, he did not like being a candidate. He loved governing, hated campaigning. Usually when I would show up at his doorstep on East Broadway, he wasn't all that thrilled to see me. Still, he never missed a stop on the trail and always worked very hard—and there were plenty of stops because I am always aggressive in booking my candidates.

George's major opposition in the primary was Jim Browning, the man who had prosecuted Patty Hearst after she joined her kidnappers in the Symbionese Liberation Army in a bank robbery. Browning seemed to have gained an advantage by supporting another ballot measure. He was pro-Proposition 13, the People's Initiative to Limit Property Taxation, authored by Howard Jarvis and Paul Gann.

It would have been politically expedient for George to support Prop 13, but he remained neutral for the simple, but honest, reason that he thought it an ill-advised measure. (George was an extremely principled politician. He had also remained neutral during the Reagan and Ford battle for the presidential nomination in 1976. This forever branded him as a liberal and surely cost him votes because Reagan was from California. He took a lot of heat for that.)

Because Browning was a formidable foe, we spent all of our money on the primary. In baseball you don't want to end a close game with your best pinch hitter on the bench. Similarly, in politics you don't want to lose the primary and be left with any money. There's always the hope/belief that you'll be able to raise more money for the general election. (One way to keep costs down? Make your office your campaign headquarters. That was the case here. Deukmejian for Attorney General operated out of the Dolphin Group's spare space in the old medical building.)

George won the June primary and faced Democrat Yvonne Brathwaite Burke, a popular African American congresswoman from Los Angeles. Here, polling—a tool that had been pioneered by Spencer-Roberts—proved invaluable. The truth is that the state attorney general doesn't deal too much with violent crime; most of the work is related to civil law or white collar criminal law. But what did the public want in an attorney general according to our polling? A tough, law and order type who'd lock up the hardcore criminals.

Congresswoman Burke didn't grasp this. She even ran a television ad in which she started out dressed as a police officer and dissolved into a suit-wearing lawyer who reminded the people that it wasn't the attorney general's job to deal with violent crime all the time, and that she'd devote herself to fighting white collar crime.

Contrast that to our pitch. We pounded home the point that Duke was tough on crime, was the father of the state's death penalty. Picture a jail cell slamming, with the tag line, "Tough, count on it."

Bill came up with the idea for what has come to be known as the *verite* spot, and Jim Rosner executed it brilliantly. Here we used actual crime victims who faced the camera and told their stories. One of my jobs was to round up twenty or so such victims to come and "audition." Then Jim picked two or three.

George was not terribly charismatic; he didn't shine in commercials. For other spots, we used powerful San Diego County Sheriff John Duffy and other law enforcement officials, members of a profession that was virtually unanimous in its support of our candidate.

How creative was Bill Roberts? With crime being a major issue, we had collected all the murder data for Los Angeles County. As a result we knew where every murder victim had been found. Bill's plan was to take scores of those big searchlights that you used to see at movie premieres, place each one at the scene of a different murder, and flip on all the switches at the same time. Of course, the press would have been alerted to take to the air in helicopters to capture the full force of the beams.

Unfortunately, we had to scrap the idea because the cost to the campaign would have been prohibitive. But that was typical of Bill's thinking. When Deukmejian ran for governor four years later, Bill created the first satellite press conference. George appeared at the Los Angeles Press Club and fielded questions from reporters in the room, as well as from reporters on satellite hookups in San Francisco, San Diego, and Sacramento. This was way back in 1982. The press was not too keen on the practice, fearing they would lose face time with candidates and politicians, but they went along with it.

I credit Bill for teaching me to think out of the box and stage big bang events to promote my own efforts. I also credit him for teaching me how important it is to maintain good relations with the media. *Always be honest with the press*, he'd tell me. *Get back to them right away, because they are on deadline and they will give you a fair shake.*

I have my share of shortcomings, but I am pretty good pitching a story, a news conference, an event, an editorial board interview—you name it. One reason for success is my effort to establish personal relationships.

There's not much I enjoy more than sitting in a bar at the end of the day, having a drink and talking politics with reporters. Journalists are smart, informed, have great stories and are fun to be around. Bill was always accessible to the press, and so am I.

Bill did have one feud with a veteran political reporter from the *Los Angeles Times*, Dick Bergholtz, the guy Richard Nixon was referring to when he uttered one of his most famous lines after losing his bid to become governor of California in 1962, "You won't have Richard Nixon to kick around anymore."

When Bill and Stu were running Reagan's first campaign for governor, Bill took Dick, an old friend, into his confidence and shared information "off the record." That's when you talk to a reporter for background only. It is an age-old way of doing business with journalists. The next day many of the Reagan campaign ideas that Bill had shared "off the record" appeared on the front page of the *Los Angeles Times*. "Don't ever call me for a story again," Bill told Dick.

The two men never talked to each other for the next eleven years until Dick was assigned to cover John Connally's campaign. Sometimes we would all be on a small plane together. Talk about awkward. Bill was loyal to a fault, but if someone double-crossed him, watch out.

***

On the same night that Californians gave the thumbs up to George Deukmejian, they gave the thumbs down to state senator John Briggs and his initiative to ban gays and lesbians from working in the state's public schools—Proposition 6. Numerous people—gay and straight—worked tirelessly to defeat Prop 6. Three deserved special recognition that evening. One was Harvey Milk, the openly gay San Francisco county supervisor. Another was political campaign consultant David Mixner. And the third was Ronald Reagan.

Allow me to take you back to the 1970s. Here are some important markers on the gay/lesbian timeline from that decade.

First, the good news:

In 1972, San Francisco; Ann Arbor, Michigan; and East Lansing, Michigan; passed the first homosexual rights ordinances.

In 1973, the American Psychiatric Association removed homosexuality from its Diagnostic and Statistical Manual of Mental Disorders.

In 1974, the first openly gay American, Kathy Kozachenko, was elected to public office. She won a seat on Ann Arbor's city council.

In 1975, homosexuality was legalized in California.

In 1976, Los Angeles Mayor Tom Bradley signed a proclamation establishing a Gay Pride Week in the city.

In 1977, Harvey Milk was elected county supervisor in San Francisco, becoming the third openly gay elected public official in the United States.

And now the bad news:

In 1977, beauty queen (1959 Miss America second runner-up), recording star ("Paper Roses"), Florida State Citrus Commission spokesperson ("Come to the Florida Sunshine State...."), and rabid anti-homosexual Anita Bryant led a successful campaign to repeal Dade County, Florida's Human Rights Ordinance, which had banned discrimination based on sexual orientation.

This brings us to 1978 and Proposition 6. Encouraged by Bryant's success, Arkansas and Oklahoma barred gays and lesbians from teaching in public schools. In that spirit, the Briggs Initiative called for the dismissal of any teacher "advocating, imposing, encouraging, or promoting" homosexual activity in the public schools. It was the first effort to use a ballot initiative to restrict gay and lesbian rights.

Initial polls showed that Proposition 6 had the support of 75% of the electorate. I would have loved to have played a public role in fighting the initiative, but being in the closet and a

Republican political consultant whose clients might be tarnished by associating with me, I had to proceed cautiously. Figuring that the best way to defeat the measure would be to demonstrate bipartisan opposition, I worked behind the scenes to involve my fellow GOPers. My first stop was a group in which I was already active, the moderate wing of the Los Angeles County Young Republicans (YR).

As Briggs and company were gathering signatures to put their initiative on the ballot, an anti-initiative fundraiser was scheduled at the Beverly Wilshire Hotel. Former Democratic presidential nominee George McGovern was to be the honored guest. As you might expect, the sponsors included openly gay individuals, gay and lesbian organizations, and Hollywood's progressive/liberal elite (Norman Lear, Jane Fonda, et al). Seeing this, I went to YR chairman Ron Macdonald. "We need to be involved," I said. For a $100 contribution, the YR's could be listed as a co-sponsor in the program. Ron (whom I later learned was gay) and I went to the YR board, and after hours of debate, got the votes necessary to officially oppose Prop 6. I had offered to pay the sponsorship of $100 myself, because I knew the opposition to Prop 6 had to be bipartisan. This would be the first official Republican opposition to what would eventually become Prop 6.

Our participation was actually quite risky for us as closeted gays and for the group. This was primarily a gay and lesbian event and was certainly associated with the Democrats. Indeed, a rival Young Republican faction in Los Angeles County, much more conservative than we were, stridently supported the Briggs Initiative and criticized our position. The press picked up the story. Ron was a trooper, frequently appearing on the local news for about two weeks to defend our position as the drama played out. What a hero.

I remember going to the fundraiser with a mixture of pride that I'd helped make the event bipartisan, exhilaration that from the podium McGovern acknowledged our participation, and fear that my secret would somehow be revealed because I was at a primarily gay event. I was scared, and I remained in the shadows that night.

I remained in the shadows after the initiative garnered enough signatures to qualify for the November ballot, but I also remained in the fight. David Mixner and his business partner Peter Scott were the leaders of the No on 6 campaign. I approached David, telling him I was gay and of my desire to help—but only behind the scenes.

David, who remains a friend, is a fascinating, brilliant person. In 1969, when in his early twenties, he was one of the organizers of the Moratorium to End the War in Vietnam. A few years later he was doing political work and organizing in Los Angeles. In 1976, he helped found the Municipal Elections Committee of Los Angeles (MECLA), the first gay and lesbian Political Action Committee in the country. At the same time, he was managing Mayor Tom Bradley's reelection effort.

Throughout the Prop 6 campaign, when any Republicans interested in helping the No campaign approached David, he directed them to me. Then I would meet with them. Some of these people were also closeted gays and lesbians. (One of the alleged gay men with whom I met after work one night at the Old World

Restaurant in Westwood would later marry, run for the top position in the California Republican Party, and win.)

Keeping the lines of communication open between Democrats and Republicans, trying to maintain some semblance of bipartisanship, proved invaluable in defeating the initiative. Who better to bestow the stamp of bipartisanship than Reagan?

Former Reagan staffers and former boyfriends Marty Dyer and Dennis Hunt approached public relations man Pete Hannaford, a top aide to Reagan during his governorship and run for president in 1976. Pete agreed to set up a meeting with Reagan for Mixner and Scott. They were forewarned that Reagan would not oppose Prop 6. To the surprise of everybody, however, the former governor agreed to do just that.

First, Reagan issued a letter saying he was against the initiative. Then he affirmed that position when answering reporters' questions. And finally, on November 1, just six days before the election, he wrote an editorial in the *Los Angeles Herald Examiner*. "Whatever else it is, homosexuality is not a contagious disease like the measles. Prevailing scientific opinion is that an individual's sexuality is determined at a very early age and that a child's teachers do not really influence this," he proclaimed.

Opposing the initiative was not the politically expedient action for a man committed to seeking his party's presidential nomination in 1980. It would have been easy for Reagan to stay on the sidelines. But he courageously followed his heart. In doing so, he made it so much easier for his fellow Republicans to vote no on 6. Support for Prop 6 before Reagan opposed it was 61% to 31%. The polling flipped after he came out against Prop 6, and the initiative ended up being defeated, 59% to 41%. (Over the years, I have taken a lot of heat over Reagan and his presidency, particularly because of his record on HIV/AIDS. I cannot defend him, nor will I; it was shameful. But people need to know that he did do some good things; opposing Prop 6 was a bold move to take when he was planning on running for president just two years later.)

To the north of us up in San Francisco, Harvey Milk was leading the opposition to Proposition 6. Milk's story is fairly well known thanks to Dustin Lance Black's brilliant 2008 movie starring Sean Penn. Born in 1930, Milk had moved from New York to San Francisco in the late 1960s. Eventually he built up a following as the unofficial Mayor of Castro Street, and after a couple of unsuccessful runs for office was elected to the San Francisco Board of Supervisors in January of 1978. (He would be assassinated less than eleven months later.)

Almost immediately after his election, Milk became embroiled in the battle over Proposition 6. He and initiative sponsor Briggs debated the proposition in several venues. At San Francisco's Gay Freedom Day Parade, a crowd estimated to be somewhere around 300,000 heard Milk deliver his "Hope Speech":

On this anniversary of Stonewall, I ask my gay sisters and brothers to make the commitment to fight. For themselves, for their freedom, for their country.... We will not win our rights by staying quietly in our closets.... We are coming out to fight the lies, the myths, the distortions. We are coming out to tell the truths about gays, for I am tired of the conspiracy of silence, so I'm going to talk about it. And I want you to talk about it. You must come out. Come out to your parents, your relatives.

Despite the encouraging development that Proposition 6 would be defeated by a million votes, I couldn't follow this exhortation—with my parents, my relatives, or my fellow workers.

Dear Mr. Karger,

I am a 16-year-old, openly gay high school sophomore in San Antonio, Texas. I would like to personally thank you so much for running for president. I completely agree with your views and morals and I would absolutely vote for you if I could. I will, however, try to convince my parents to vote for you with all of my willpower. Thank you for giving me hope that one day I will be able to marry the person I love. Thank you also

for being an inspiration to people everywhere. I wish you the best of luck on your journey and I hope you succeed in all.

Sincerely,

A.

CHAPTER SIX

"YOUNG MAN, GET BACK HERE."

November 4, 1980. A friend and I are at the Century Plaza Hotel on Los Angeles's Avenue of the Stars. The star tonight is Ronald Reagan, who has handily defeated the incumbent President Jimmy Carter. Our firm has done some work on the campaign, but my friend and I are by no means part of the inner circle. We have managed to get into the "friends and family" reception in a meeting room off of the main ballroom.

There are, perhaps, one hundred people here. We are witnesses to history, right up front for Reagan's first speech as President-elect. Nancy and all four of his children are behind him.

After the inspiring talk concludes, we wander around some of the other rooms. My friend spies a huge sheet cake in the shape of a map of the United States. "Let's present this to him," he says.

We each lift up one side of the cake. "I don't think so," I say, and leave the room. I head off by myself to a small press room with several TV monitors, all of which are tuned in to the main ballroom, where the President-elect is now a few minutes into his victory speech to the nation. The ballroom is packed with several thousand supporters and hundreds of reporters. The television networks are broadcasting live. It's quite a moment.

The next thing I know, out come my friend and a bald guy carrying the cake. Reagan is still speaking. When the cake carriers approach him, the crowd cheers. Nancy Reagan glares at the two. My pal steps up to the microphone and says, "Mr. President-elect, we want to present you with this cake of the United States. The flags represent the states that you carried tonight." (There were some little American flags on toothpicks randomly stuck in various states.)

Just then the two tilt the cake toward the cameras. *How's that cake staying on the platter*? I think. I wonder if there are small wooden pegs to secure it in place. In that split second of thought, the cake starts to slide. The surprised carriers quickly right it. And without missing a beat, Ronald Reagan says, "Just when I get elected the country starts to fall apart."

What a line. The crowd cheers. My friend and his co-conspirator exit stage left.

***

Most people would agree that the country didn't fall apart during the eight years that Ronald Reagan was president. 1981-1988 was a pretty good time for America. It was also a pretty good time for the Dolphin Group.

Let me back up a bit. As I've noted, political consulting firms often experience lean times in between elections. Fortunately, after the Deukmejian victory of 1978, we kept ourselves pretty busy by working on behalf of two very different commercial clients involved in high profile disputes. Then in the second half of 1979, we were hired by a front-runner for the Republican nomination for president—and it wasn't Ronald Reagan.

The Dolphin Group had previously worked with each of the two commercial clients. California farmers had retained the firm in 1976 to fight Proposition 14—the matter for which Bill had initially

94

wanted to hire me. The growers didn't forget Bill's success in defeating that initiative to write the Agricultural Labor Relations Act into the state Constitution. In 1979 the Imperial Valley lettuce growers and Cesar Chavez's United Farm Workers (UFW) could not reach an agreement on a new contract, and the UFW went on strike. The vegetable growers hired us to manage what was, in effect, their "campaign" to prevail in their contest with Chavez and the union.

On the day we were retained, Lee and I got on an airplane to meet with the growers in the Imperial Valley. Soon I had relocated to the small farming town of El Centro, to direct the press operation during the strike. As Chavez was a charismatic national figure and this was the height of the winter lettuce season, the strike was a big story attracting national media right off the bat. The farmers needed to tell their side of the story.

Chavez was not only charismatic, he was sympathetic. The media clearly liked him, and the UFW's David vs. Goliath-type tale made for good headlines. Initially, not knowing too much about him, I, too, was a fan. I remembered that a few of my friends' parents had honored his grape boycott a decade earlier.

My job, however, was to represent Goliath. And to do so, I had to be in Goliath's front yard. In January 1979, I moved into the run-down Airporter Motel. As the name implies, it was right next to the Imperial County Airport in El Centro. The runway was a couple hundred feet away. I lived there for the next three months, coming home only on weekends and having a difficult time, mostly due to the isolation.

I don't want to ruin any romantic notions about Cesar Chavez, but on the ground I saw that this supposedly non-violent labor leader was inciting decidedly violent behavior. I am not saying that he ordered such activity; I'm saying that I saw such behavior a lot over the six months that I worked on the strike.

When the winter lettuce harvest and the strike moved up to Salinas in the spring, I was even under attack. I was at a meeting in an office just outside of town when striking farm workers stormed and attacked the compound. As rocks and bottles flew, some farmers rushed me up some stairs to a little office away from the main building and told me to hide under a desk.

Early on I was provided around-the-clock security because we had received so many threats. A former sheriff's deputy was assigned to protect me. He slept in the room next to me at the Airporter and drove me to work each day. He'd guard the office when I was there. It was a pretty scary time.

Fearful and homesick, I took solace when Dolphin Group partners would come for periodic meetings. "Take me home with you," I'd plead, only half facetiously.

Still, this was a great learning experience for a young man just starting out in the business. I constantly dealt with local and national media, and I watched as Bill came up with one creative plan after another. One example: Volunteer Harvest Day. Shortly after the strike started, the growers invited friends, family, and supporters to step in for the striking workers and cut the lettuce. It was actually on my twenty-ninth birthday, January 31, 1979.

All three networks (only CBS, NBC, and ABC then) flew in to cover Harvest Day. It was a media frenzy, a made-for-TV event.

As volunteers cut lettuce, cameramen and reporters literally ran all around the beautiful fields to get their shots.

Because they weren't paid, these volunteers weren't scabs as the UFW alleged. True, they didn't do a terribly professional job and much of their harvest could not be used. But we made the point that if the lettuce weren't harvested at all, the whole crop would be lost, driving prices up across the country.

Afraid of losing their crop, the growers did bring in replacement workers. This led to increased violence—overturned buses, broken windows, roads sabotaged to flatten the tires of the buses carrying the replacements. We responded peacefully, running full-page ads throughout the state showing photographs of the attacks. We would also hold press conferences in Los Angeles and in other cities around California to allow the victims of the violence to tell firsthand what had happened.

Up to this point Cesar Chavez—whose heart, I still believe, was in the right place—could do no wrong in the eyes of the public. While he served a great purpose in bettering the conditions for hundreds of thousands of farm workers all over the country, things had gone awry this time. When those workers' actions were different from his non-violent words, we called them and him out on it.

Still, it wasn't easy to make our case. In the battle of Chavez vs. California Agriculture, Chavez had the public and press in his corner. That's one reason we ran ads in order to tell the farmers' side of the story. We took our message right to the public.

I have long been a believer in bipartisanship and have made it a cornerstone in my talks as I run for the presidency. So lest my progressive friends think that the Dolphin Group and I were always on the side of business, I must describe our work at this time on behalf of the second client I mentioned above. Here, in league with a coalition of environmentalists, Native Americans, activists, and others, we took on Pacific Gas & Electric and Southern California Gas, the two utilities that controlled California's energy supply.

Our involvement began when we received a call from the Bixby Ranch Company, which owned Point Conception, a 25,000-acre plot of land north of Santa Barbara right on the Pacific Ocean. The utilities wanted to build a Liquefied Natural Gas (LNG) facility just south of the property.

As the name suggests, LNG involves temporarily turning natural gas into liquid form for storage or transport. Many people in government, industry, and the not-for-profit sector justifiably champion natural gas as an alternative to oil. At the same time, the safety of the extraction, liquefaction, and gasification processes has justifiably been called into question. Is too much harmful carbon dioxide and nitrogen oxide being released? Is the site in the most feasible (safest) place? Santa Barbara had already experienced a terrible oil spill in 1969. No one wanted another environmental disaster.

By the time we were enlisted, much of the progressive community had started organizing (or had remained organized from the spill ten years earlier). Our allies included the Sierra Club, Get Oil Out (GOO), and most other prominent environmental groups. The Chumash Indians were also involved. Point Conception was a sacred site to them, the "Western Gate," where the soul passed from this world to the next—not the place where gas should pass from liquid.

Lee headed up what was one of the most enjoyable campaigns on which I've ever worked. We were able to wear blue jeans instead of suits. The people in our coalition were fun to be around. Jackson Browne gave concerts. And it didn't hurt that for once, in the eyes of the press and most of the public, we were the good guys.

Nearly every politician supported the LNG facility. Even the liberal Jerry Brown, who was serving his second term as governor of California, backed it (perhaps, some suggested, because his father was a partner in Pertamina Oil, which was the project's major investor). If you've read this far, you know that I enjoy taking on the establishment. This was the first time I'd done that with the Dolphin Group, and it was a kick.

(In the political consulting business, it's not all that unusual to see Republican consultants and Democratic consultants on the same team. We're not nearly as partisan as politicians. This does not mean we are unprincipled. Just like lawyers, we often take on clients with different points of view. As I said in one of my early commercials in New Hampshire, I've learned that by working with both sides, getting along with people, forming alliances, you can get things done. Sadly, too many of today's politicians— establishment and anti-establishment—don't get it.)

I was dividing my time between the exhilarating Point Conception project and the difficult Imperial Valley, when Dolphin snared another client—John Connally. The 62-year-old former Democrat who had served as governor of Texas, secretary of the

Navy (under President Kennedy), and secretary of the Treasury (under President Nixon) was, along with Ronald Reagan, considered a frontrunner for the Republican nomination for president.

Bill's hard and fast rule was never to solicit candidates because, as he would say, "then you have to justify your existence." In this instance he broke his rule for two reasons. First, he really wanted a piece of the 1980 presidential campaign action. Stu Spencer had managed a presidential bid—Ford in 1976—but Bill had yet to do so.

The second and more important reason? Bill was absolutely convinced that Connally was the right guy for the times. This was a critical period in U.S. / Soviet relations. Bill knew Reagan just about better than anyone and didn't think he was tough enough to deal with the Russians. Connally's hawkish stance, on the other hand, was well known. In Bill's eyes, we needed a tough son-of-a-bitch who wouldn't let the USSR get away with anything.

Initially, Dolphin Group was hired to coordinate the Connally primary effort in the six western states. Bill was also named to Connally's strategy team that met regularly in Washington, D.C. But he had his eye on a bigger prize—running the entire campaign. (For Connally, I would argue, there was no bigger prize than getting Bill. The Texan could brag that one of Reagan's top advisors had chosen to work for him.)

Initially Bill and I were the only Dolphin Group members tasked to the campaign. My title was "Deputy Campaign Director and Communications Director, Western United States." Whenever the governor came west, Bill and I would hop on his airplane, usually Southern Pacific's G-3, and accompany him to his appearances that we had arranged. Mrs. Connally was often on board, as were a variety of political operatives. Connally's western states finance chairmen—Southern Pacific's CEO Ben Biagginni and president Alan Furth—were usually present.

At twenty-nine, I was the youngest team member by far. Connally had a press secretary, the affable Jim Brady. Jim, who, tragically, would later be shot while serving President Reagan, often made the western swing. But on these trips, the scheduling of press conferences was my responsibility. As you might imagine, it was a lot easier to get the media's attention for such events than it had been when working on the state attorney general's race for George Deukmejian.

The governor was tough. I saw him lose his temper a couple times. Once a junior reporter showed up late for a press conference in San Diego. "I'm sorry," he said timidly.

"You're late!" Connally bellowed. "Everybody else got here on time! I'm not going to give you an interview!" Poor guy. Thankfully, I never had a problem.

Connally made five or six western trips for two or three days each. I briefed him, went to the press conferences, and attended organizational meetings and fundraising meetings— including one where a dozen or so heavy hitters flew in on their own jets for a meeting in a cheap, tiny Holiday Inn we'd found near the airport. The room we met in was so small that every time someone got up to go to the bathroom, you'd hear it all. We could even tell if someone washed his hands or not. The Dolphin Group was notoriously frugal on all our campaigns.

Connally, of course, didn't last long enough in the race to run in any of the primaries in our bailiwick, the west. George H.W. Bush was the surprise winner in Iowa. Then Reagan won in New Hampshire. South Carolina and Florida were next. Bill was asked to go down to Florida and salvage the state for the governor as he had for President Ford. Dolphin Group advertising director Jim Rosner and I went with him for a couple of weeks. Unfortunately, we never were able to see the fruits of our last minute effort. After losing badly in South Carolina, Connally withdrew from the campaign two days before the primary in the Sunshine State.

What began as the best-financed campaign was a disaster. The amount of money spent and the return on investment has been immortalized by pundits, who referred to the lone supporter obligated to Connally as "the $10 million delegate." Would it have been different if Bill had been national campaign director? I definitely think so.

One final note about this campaign and the lot of the political consultants in general. Sometimes the candidate runs out of money and doesn't pay his or her bills, including the consultants' time and expenses. The well-heeled Connally campaign stiffed us. After repeated attempts to collect, Bill prevailed on a commercial client who was also a friend of Connally to plead our case several years later. We ended up settling for about two-thirds of our bill. Many others who worked on that campaign weren't so lucky. One friend of mine went to Iowa on the governor's behalf. "Put your expenses on your credit card," he was told. He did and was never reimbursed. Terrible.

Having worked for Ford in 1976 and Connally in 1980, Bill was not on Reagan's good side as he had been when managing the gubernatorial efforts years earlier. But thanks to Stu Spencer, who was serving as campaign director, the Dolphin Group played a minor role in the general election versus President Carter. We bought ads in California and a few other states for Reagan/Bush.

I went to the convention in Detroit. Thanks to friends who were in charge of orchestrating the event, I often had the best seat in the house. I spent half my time helping out where needed and the other half going to parties. Given various all-access credentials by good friend Gary Hunt each day, I could go down to the convention floor and up to the skyboxes. Most evenings I was in the Republican Senatorial Campaign Committee box with distinguished guests such as Elizabeth Taylor, who was married to U.S. Senator John Warner at the time.

One month after the near fiasco with the cake on election night, I took a chance. Just two years into my stint at the Dolphin Group, I asked Bill Roberts if I could go to Washington, D.C., to work on the Reagan inauguration. My good friend Marty Dyer was heading the committee that would handle arrangements for those governors who would be attending. He had told me there was a volunteer position open. Since I'd always wanted to spend time in Washington (and in the back of my mind I had been thinking about looking for a job in the new administration), I was excited.

What kind of job? I wasn't sure. But I left for D.C. in late November 1980.

As it turned out, I actually got paid to work on the inauguration. Not a lot. But any pay was a bonus. I roomed with three other office mates—Marty; a good friend from L.A., Meade Camp; and a recently divorced friend of Marty's who was just coming out. We lived in the Columbia Plaza Apartment complex across the street from the far more famous Watergate.

There were six guys working in the Governors, State, and Local Officials Participation Office, and all of us were gay. Our four cute female assistants were all straight. They would sometimes comment that we were so "polite," since we never hit on them.

We had a blast, but I never worked so hard in my life. We handled all the inaugural arrangements for forty-six governors, including tickets, hotels, and transportation. Each governor got a military aide, a driver, and other perks.

I especially recall dealing with two very different types of governor. California's Jerry Brown—known for a monastic lifestyle that included sleeping on a mattress on the floor of his spartan apartment in Sacramento—decided to come at the last minute. We had to scramble to get him tickets because his office hadn't cooperated with our office at all.

And then there was Texas Governor Bill Clements. He sent a wonderful guy from his political operation, Herb Butrum, to Washington for almost two months just to make his arrangements. The governor wanted to fly in his personal limousine from Austin for the festivities. These were tough economic times. Austerity was the inauguration mantra. We talked the Texan out of that excess.

My friends and I went to many of the pre-inauguration parties. We had made lots of new friends and connections after working at the Inaugural Committee for two months. Immediately following the opening ceremony at the Lincoln Memorial, we sought refuge from the freezing temperature and ended up at the State Department party for Vice President Bush. It was held in the Diplomatic Reception Rooms on the top floor of Foggy Bottom.

On Inauguration Day our jobs were over, and I ended up in the Capitol Building behind the proceedings. Knowing a little about how to meet celebrities, I positioned myself as President Reagan and company came inside immediately after the oath of office was administered. I think I was one of the first people to call him "Mr. President," as I shook his hand. He did a double-take because he wasn't yet accustomed to being addressed in that manner. (I spent the next ten years trying to get a picture of that moment, but never could find one.)

The next day I attended a party that President and Mrs. Reagan gave at the White House for close friends, inauguration department heads, and top administration officials. I was none of the above, of course, but I really wanted to go. Seeing the memo in our department about the party, I had called in advance to add two names to the list, a co-worker's and mine—both deputy directors of the department. We waited in a long line to get in, unsure if our names were on the list. They were.

What a star-studded cocktail party! Bob Hope was there, as was Johnny Carson. Actress and World War II pinup girl Betty Grable was also present. She posed with me for a picture that I still have.

As much as I liked the Washington party scene, I was by this time convinced I did not want to work there. I'd seen too much backstabbing, too much red tape. And the weather couldn't compare with Los Angeles. Exhausted, I was planning to go to Key

West and then back to California when Bill called. "Young man," he said, "get back here." Attorney General George Deukmejian was considering running for governor in 1982 and wanted to set up an exploratory committee.

***

I do not intend to deliver a blow by blow of every political campaign in which I was involved in my twenty-seven years at the Dolphin Group. But the two campaigns I worked on in advance of the 1982 elections warrant some description—Deukmejian for Governor and Reagan for U.S. Senator. That's Maureen Reagan, of course, the daughter of the president and his first wife, actress Jane Wyman.

I'll start with Maureen. She hired us five days before she announced she was running. We organized a statewide fly-around for announcement day, and I accompanied her and her husband Dennis Revell on the plane to press conferences in four cities. On this trip and subsequent trips, the Secret Service would meet us and provide transportation and security. (It's the only way to go!) Protection tripled after Libya's Muammar Gaddafi threatened the lives of the Reagan children.

Maureen was about forty at this time. She'd had a rough life. She was a tough woman, incredibly bright and articulate.

The White House was not excited about her bid, which, of course, attracted tremendous media attention. They feared her run would be viewed as a referendum on her father's presidency just two years into his term. I felt sorry for her because she wasn't taken as seriously as she should have been. She had her peculiarities. After each press conference on her announcement fly-around, we'd get back on the plane and she would pull out a beat-up hand puppet and put it on.

Correct. She kept a puppet—a little dog—in her purse. Like a little girl, she would carry on a conversation with it to pump herself up.

This was a wide-open primary. Maureen was the only woman in the field. A reporter dubbed the race "Snow White and the Seven Dwarves." Unfortunately, Snow White's campaign was soon laid to rest. Pete Wilson won the primary and then the general election in November.

I spent more of my time with George Deukmejian than Maureen. He was involved in a tough primary battle with Ronald Reagan protégé Mike Curb. Mike, a truly nice guy, was already a successful record company owner when he ran for lieutenant governor in 1978 and won. Considered more conservative and much better known than Deukmejian, he held the early lead in the primary. But he faltered after an intemperate public outburst or two. After word leaked out that he had never voted until he ran for lieutenant governor, he was never able to recover. (That helpful tidbit came to me from Bill Barnes, a reporter with the *San Francisco Examiner*, who suggested checking Mike's voting record.)

George's opponent in the general election was popular Los Angeles Mayor Tom Bradley. With the important support of a most gracious Mike Curb who helped to unify a fractured Republican Party, Duke ended up winning by 93,000 votes out of the 7.5 million cast. Sadly, we were not with him the last three weeks to truly celebrate his victory. Why? Three infamous words: *the Bradley Effect.*

Despite George's victory, 1982 was not a particularly good year for Bill Roberts. First, he lost a couple of toes due to diabetes. Then, just three weeks before the November election, he spoke the truth and suffered the consequences. I was in the room when it happened, so here is the inside story:

In mid-October polls showed Bradley about five to seven percentage points ahead of Deukmejian. We had made some new commercials for the stretch run and invited reporters to our office for a screening. Three or four came.

Bradley was attempting to become the first African American to win a governor's race in the history of the United States

At the screening, the reporters wanted to know how Duke could overcome Bradley's sizable lead in just three weeks. Bill responded that it was still possible to win; we just needed to close strong. Then, after much prodding from the reporters, he noted that the polls might not be accurate, that people aren't always honest when they are taking a survey over the phone.

"What does that mean?" asked the reporters.

Bill tried to leave it at that, but the reporters kept pushing. Well, Bill elaborated, they're lifelong Democrats and they're not going to reveal on the phone that they are voting Republican, lest they be thought of as prejudiced.

Uh-oh. I knew the moment he said it that we were in trouble. The reporters were excited. They all left with what they knew was a big story. I went into Lee's office and told him what had happened.

It didn't take long for the headlines to appear—not just in California, but around the country—and for the shoe to drop. The Deukmejian campaign asked us to resign. We did.

And so it was that after orchestrating an upset victory over Mike Curb in the primary and a dramatic comeback in the general against Tom Bradley, the Dolphin Group was not on hand to celebrate Duke's comeback. Interestingly, the victory was explained as the Bradley Effect. The polls had been wrong because people who said they were voting for Bradley hadn't planned to. Bill knew that all along.

Some observers thought Bill had been calculating; it was all a plan to make people think twice about voting for Bradley or to give them cover to vote for Deukmejian. No. He had simply been honest.

Bill the gourmand loved to go out for a big dinner. Since we were not busy on this particular election night, what better way to take the edge off what had been a tense day. Since the Dolphin Group was *firm non grata* at Deukmejian headquarters, he took three of us to Chasen's, where we had one of the most expensive options on the menu, the seafood sampler. There, we listened to results on transistor radios.

I had worn a suit to dinner, thinking that if Duke won I might wander over to the Century Plaza for the celebration. (Bill had no interest.) Initially, however, the press declared Bradley the winner. I went home.

Later in the evening, there was a new declaration. Deukmejian had won. I'd changed out of my suit. Now I put it back on and headed to the hotel. "Awkward" best describes how it felt to be part of the celebration. Still it was nice to see so many of the people I had worked with over the last twenty-plus months. I felt I'd played a significant role in reaching the evening's happy result and wanted to be a part of the festivities.

***

Election night at the Century Plaza two years later had all the fun and none of the awkwardness of 1982. Reagan/Bush had been reelected in a landslide. Despite Bill's up and down history with the Reagan camp, the Dolphin Group had been heavily involved in the campaign, and (except for one unfortunate evening) I'd had the time of my life throughout all of 1984.

Let's back up. Although Ed Rollins was officially the campaign manager and public face of Reagan/Bush '84, Stu Spencer was the behind-the-scenes strategist. Aware, obviously, of the talents of Bill and Dolphin, he made sure we were involved, helping us get contracts with the Republican National Committee (RNC) and the Reagan/Bush campaign.

One of our jobs was to travel to Texas and tamp out the still smoldering tensions between Reagan loyalists and Bush loyalists. But the main task in our portfolio was opposition research. Long before the Democrats settled on Walter Mondale, we began looking at all the possible nominees—Gary Hart, Jesse Jackson, John Glenn, and others. Bill and I frequently flew to Washington, D.C., to meet with the campaign braintrust—Rollins, Lyn Nofziger, and a young South Carolinian named Lee Atwater.

Lee, whom I would come to know better, was creative, energetic, partisan, and simply brilliant. All credit to Stu for recognizing Lee's potential and finding the right niche for him.

The campaign results were pretty much a foregone conclusion regardless of whom the Democrats nominated. But it was exciting to be in the Reagan war room and gratifying to see how much Bill was revered. I worked closely with the number two guy at the RNC, Bill Greener. Every Saturday morning I led a conference call discussion about the shortcomings of the Democratic candidates.

We knew about these shortcomings thanks to the RNC's brand new research ability—a computerized database on all the leading Democrats running for president that year. Revolutionary back in 1984, this database had all their votes, quotes, and information. Tens of thousands of newspaper stories alone were easily accessible. Our job working for the RNC during the primaries was to get that information out to the media and the public.

Bill came up with an ingenious way to share this information with the world. Remember, this was 1984, long before the universal use of the Internet, YouTube, Facebook, campaign web pages, Twitter, CNN, MSNBC, and Fox News.

The idea? The Republican Fact and Information Store. Picture a trade show booth with a computer and terminal, circa 1984. Within our three cardboard walls—a real pain to lug around—we weren't selling cars or toys or restaurant gadgets. We were giving away the skinny on all the Democrats. And we weren't set up at trade shows but, rather, the sites of the Democratic debates.

Our target audience was the press. Want to know how Hart voted on the tax bill two years ago? Are you aware what Mondale said about the Soviet Union when he first ran for senator in Minnesota? We had all this and more in our computer. Sounds so standard now, but Bill was so far ahead of his time.

After it became apparent that former Vice President Mondale was going to be the nominee, the fun really started. I was tasked to put together a speakers bureau composed of high profile Republicans and Democrats willing to travel the country and extol Reagan (and criticize Mondale so that the president could remain, well, presidential, above the fray).

Our only restriction: don't use anyone with a title in the Reagan/Bush campaign. RNC operations were a separate matter. If, for example, a governor or senator were state chairman of the reelection effort, he or she was taboo. Still, with the help of a crew that included Duke Blackwood (who now heads the Reagan Library) in Washington, DC; Peter McKenzie in Dallas; Lauren Zanca in Chicago; and Dolphin in Los Angeles, we ran a national campaign for the RNC.

We assembled an impressive stable of advocates: Indiana senators Richard Lugar and Dan Quayle; Carla Hills, who had been secretary of Housing and Urban Development under President Ford; and even a Democrat whose name I can't recall who had been an ambassador in the Carter-Mondale administration. Thanks to wealthy benefactors like former Postmaster General Red

Blount, these advocates often flew on borrowed private jets from city to city praising Reagan and pointing out Mondale's negatives.

And then there was my favorite speaker—the one I worked the hardest to sign up and the one whom I accompanied on numerous stops along the trail over several weeks: Arizona Senator Barry Goldwater. He'd beaten my guy Nelson Rockefeller for the Republican nomination twenty years earlier and still was more conservative than I on many issues, but by now he was one of my heroes—a straight shooter who stood on his principles.

After weeks of cajoling Goldwater's chief of staff Judy Eisenhower, I got the news that the senator would join the team. We quickly booked speaking engagements and lots of media for the iconic statesman.

We treated Goldwater royally. I went everywhere with him. As he was seventy-five years old and had a bad hip, we tried to make life as comfortable as possible for him. We flew most places on the private jet of real estate mogul and San Diego Chargers owner Alex Spanos, one of the richest men in America.

Usually the senator and I were the only two passengers, pampered by a beautiful flight attendant who plied us with bakery goods from Mr. Spanos's favorite hometown Stockton bakery. On our first trip, I finagled a big limousine from Orange County industrialist Bob Fluor to take us to the airport.

"A sedan is more than adequate," the senator barked. It was easier to get in and out of. After that I would just pick him up in my car.

In 1964, the Republicans had held their convention in San Francisco. As Mondale was to be anointed by the Democrats in the same city, we wanted Goldwater there. He agreed and for three days in San Francisco he spoke to the press formally and informally. Cary Davidson, a young University of Chicago Law School graduate who is now my lawyer, did a great job of writing the senator's speeches and talking points for these appearances.

I would have liked it if the senator took off the gloves a bit more. But that wasn't his style at this time. He chose to win people over with wit and humor.

As a political junkie, I was in heaven. We hit it off, and he shared stories and philosophy with me. One time I summoned my courage and said, "Senator, I'm puzzled. You have great conservative credentials, yet you're pro-choice." (As am I.)

He looked over the top of his glasses and said, "Young man, when your wife is president of Planned Parenthood of Arizona, you, too, are pro-choice!"

I had different experiences at the two conventions in 1984. In San Francisco, I managed to sneak onto the floor after saying good night to Senator Goldwater. There I ran into Linda Breakstone, a reporter friend from the *Los Angeles Herald Examiner*. "What are you doing down here?" she asked, shaking her head.

Duke Blackwood and I manned the Fact and Information Store at the Republican convention in Dallas. Bill didn't come, so I was able to use his invitations to several parties where I met the likes of Walter Cronkite, Sam Donaldson, and Chris Wallace. My assignment from Bill was to get the signatures of all the men and women featured in his beautiful leather-bound book of President Reagan's first cabinet. The book was produced by Citizens for the

Republic (CFTR), Reagan's PAC started with leftover campaign funds after he was elected. CFTR was our client, and its executive director, Curtis Mack, had proudly presented one to Bill.

While in Dallas for my fourth consecutive convention, I crashed a couple of parties. One too many, in fact. After enjoying myself at a New Mexico delegation party held at some petroleum club on the top floor of a high-rise office building, I was mugged as I walked back to my hotel.

Later I remembered two guys in jogging suits approaching as I walked down Acker Street ... and then waking up disoriented in the gutter, a bloody and aching mess. My wallet and watch were gone, but my money clip was still in my pocket.

Rising unsteadily, I flagged down a taxi. Seeing my beaten face, the driver started to take off. Fortunately, I showed him my money and he took me to the Fairmont Hotel. Security approached me when I walked into the lobby, presumably to throw me out, but after realizing that I was a hotel guest, they instantly took control and helped me. They called the paramedics, who took me to the hospital.

My upper lip and ear got the worst of it. When the doctor came out to stitch me up, I gave him the line Reagan had used on his surgeon after being shot in 1981: "I hope you're a Republican."

Eight stitches later, I was quite a sight. In pain and unpresentable, I went back to the hotel and gave away the hottest ticket in town—a floor pass to the convention the next night, the evening that Reagan would accept the nomination. Later a photographer from the *Dallas Morning News* found my wallet by a

Dumpster. If only the thugs had asked me for money before they started hitting me. I would have gladly complied.

Weeks later I was in a lot better shape than the Mondale-Ferraro campaign. President Reagan was poised to win all fifty states. Only Massachusetts and Minnesota were still in play.

Seeking an unprecedented sweep, Reagan/Bush dispatched teams to the two states. Dolphin Group was given Minnesota, Mondale's home state. Bill came up with the idea of taking a poll in the precinct in which Mondale lived. It wasn't terribly risky. This was an affluent neighborhood, largely Republican. The poll showed Reagan with a three to one edge. Demoralizing for the Democrats. Great press coverage for Reagan/Bush.

Bill also lobbied for a surprise visit by the president. On the eve of the election, Reagan flew into Mondale territory and held a big airport rally in Minneapolis. On election night he carried Minnesota and forty-eight other states.

The president's people should have sent Bill to Massachusetts, too.

Dear Mr. Karger,

I am an 18-year-old gay male from Pennsylvania, and I would like to applaud your courage and bravery in running for president. I know that you obviously have much more life under your belt than I, but I definitely know how hard it is, and being gay can definitely complicate anything in our society.

I think it is great that you are standing up for what you believe is right, and for this I would like to thank you for being someone I can look up to, someone that I can hope to be as great as. You have given me hope that there will be a better tomorrow....

The dawn is rising over the world, and you are leading the way. Congratulations, because in my regard, you have already won. I do want to state that it is not only because of this one issue that I will support you. Of course it means a whole hell of a lot to me but I have watched your interviews and videos, and I appreciate your ideas and views on a lot of topics. I like your idea to make an amendment to allow 17- and 16-year-olds the right to vote.

Nate

CHAPTER SEVEN

"NOW YOU KNOW WHY I GOT INTO POLITICS."

Summer 1988. Bill Roberts has succumbed to
complications from diabetes. In addition to the life example and
know-how he bequeathed to us, he has left the Dolphin Group the
idea for an organization to help Vice President George H.W. Bush
succeed Ronald Reagan. The Committee for the Presidency will
actually, *must* operate independent of the official Bush campaign.
It will raise funds, campaign on behalf of the candidate, and air
commercials. I'm able to persuade former Los Angeles Dodgers
and San Diego Padres star first baseman Steve Garvey to head the
Committee.

A few weeks into the effort, firm partner Lee Stitzenberger
comes into my office. He shows me a *Reader's Digest* article that
has just come out about the crime victims of one Willie Horton, a
murderer who had been given a furlough in Massachusetts when
the Democratic candidate Michael Dukakis was governor there. We
have extensive experience in working with such victims and
tremendous credibility in the victims' movement. "Let's see if we
can find these folks and if they're willing to get involved," he says.

It's almost a throwaway line, one of scores of ideas that we
bounce off each other every day. I immediately ask our research
director, Russ DiLando, to see if he can come up with anything. He
calls the author of the article, who puts us in touch with Horton's
victims. Before the election, the murderer will be the subject of two

sets of the most famous, controversial commercials in campaign history.

***

I've previously noted how we involved crime victims to bolster the law and order image of George Deukmejian when he ran for attorney general in 1978, and we did the same when he ran for governor in 1982. But we really earned our stripes in the years that followed. From 1983 to 1986 we coordinated an effort to vote Rose Bird, the Chief Justice of the California Supreme Court, out of office. I've tried to be judicious in selecting the campaigns I recount here. The Bird case is instructive not just because it sowed the seeds for our Horton-related commercials in 1988, but because it demonstrates how to put together a bipartisan group for a cause. Here's how I remember it:

At some point in 1983, the Dolphin Group was approached by three men wishing to oust Chief Justice Bird, who had been the subject of much controversy from the moment Governor Jerry Brown nominated her in 1977. Opponents of that nomination noted that she was being asked to lead the state's highest court even though she had never been a judge at any level. She had been Brown's campaign driver, a public defender, and a law professor, and her stances with respect to crime led law enforcement to oppose her. She had also been Brown's secretary of agriculture and had alienated growers who thought her far too liberal and board members who questioned her administrative abilities.

A California Supreme Court justice must be confirmed by the electorate in the first general election ballot after he or she is appointed and reconfirmed each time when his or her term is up.

An effort to vote out Bird in 1978 had failed. There were also several failed recall attempts. But by 1983, her rulings had antagonized enough people so that there seemed to be a good chance of defeating her in 1986 when she was up for the mandated reconfirmation.

For the most part, her unpopular and controversial rulings had to do with the death penalty. By the time the reconfirmation vote took place, she had voted to overturn the death penalty in sixty-two out of sixty-two cases. As Stanley Mosk, another liberal Supreme Court justice who was not targeted for defeat that year, would later say, "I think the death penalty is wrong, that a person has no right to kill, and the state has no right to kill. But the difference [between me and Rose Bird] is that I took an oath to support the law as it is and not as I might prefer it to be, and therefore, I've written my share of opinions upholding capital judgments."

When an unlikely trio consisting of a deputy district attorney, hay broker, and accountant approached us to help oust Bird, there was already another effort underway. But it was being led by State Senator Bill Richardson who was as far to the right as Bird was to the left. Bill Roberts determined that it was our task to put together a coalition of moderate, reasonable folks who could persuade the electorate that Bird was the wrong person to be in charge of the state's highest court. Toward that end he thought we should enlist the non-partisan crime victims with whom we had worked on Deukmejian's campaigns for attorney general and governor. Keep in mind, we weren't orchestrating a recall; those initiatives, which generally stem from malfeasance in office, had been attempted and failed. We were simply asking the people of California to vote against reconfirming the chief justice.

Initially, this was a difficult battle. The three men who had approached us had few connections and even less money. We had connections, but it's difficult to get people excited three years before a scheduled vote. Bill put together a group called Crime Victims for Court Reform. He wanted the victims, not the politicians, to lead the campaign to oust Bird. This received some publicity, but what we really needed was cash to mount a campaign.

Enter two financial angels. The first was Dick Riordan. Dick would eventually serve as Mayor of Los Angeles from 1993 to 2001, but at this time he was a political neophyte. (He graciously credits me with getting him into the arena.) I was managing the Crime Victims' campaign in 1984, when Dick called, referred by powerful political attorney Chip Nielsen. We'd get a lot of calls every day, and I offered Dick my usual response. I would send him some information.

He then said, "Let me tell you a little bit about myself ... I am the largest shareholder of Mattel." I stopped him right there and suggested we meet. The second angel was Marshall Ezralow, a very successful real estate developer. I persuaded the two of them to become co-finance chairs.

Dick proved essential to what Bill irreverently titled (and had bumper stickers made for) the "Bye Bye Birdie" effort. He was a moderate Republican, but he had been the largest contributor to the mayoral campaign of Tom Bradley, a Democrat. Soon he brought in one of his law partners, Bill Wardlaw, a full-fledged

Democrat who had served as U.S. Senator Alan Cranston's campaign chair. A Republican L.A. County supervisor named Pete Schabarum was also a benefactor.

Now we were clearly a bipartisan effort able to give mainstream credibility to the effort. And now we called for the voters to say no to two other justices who, like Bird, overturned the death penalty in virtually every case and were also up for voter confirmation in 1986. *Let's restore the reputation of what was once considered the best supreme court in the country*, we said.

Complementing the credibility of our coalition was the credibility and appeal of our main spokespersons, the crime victims themselves. In the mid-1980s, the victims' movement was still in its infancy. Ellen Dunne, the ex-wife of writer Dominick Dunne, had formed Justice for Homicide Victims after her daughter Dominique had been murdered in 1982. She was a tireless advocate. We worked with her and many other victim organizations. We also sought out the families of all the victims in the cases in which Bird had overturned the death penalty.

Most of these families ended up participating. They would fly or drive into Los Angeles for group meetings at which they would share their heartbreaking stories and hear from speakers. These were really "group therapy sessions."

Until getting to know these brave men and women, I had opposed the death penalty. That changed after I saw how much their lives had been altered forever. They'd gone through hell by losing loved ones, only to be further tormented in the court system. Many of these cases had gone on for over ten or fifteen years, with trial after trial and appeal after appeal and, finally, what seemed like the blind overturning of the death penalty by Bird and Justices Cruz Reynoso and Joseph Grodin. The only way a family could get closure was to know that the assailant of their loved one would receive the ultimate penalty. This was the most emotional campaign on which I ever worked.

We ran commercials and some of the victims spoke at press conferences. Not wanting to appear insensitive, reporters would often preface their questions with: "Let me play devil's advocate...."

Governor Deukmejian was running for reelection himself. He, of course, opposed Bird, Reynoso, and Grodin, but was not involved in our campaign. When he was attorney general, he and Bird and an appellate judge had served on the state commission that evaluated judicial nominations. I had attended some of these meetings, and Duke's distaste for Bird was palpable. He had opposed recall efforts, but now looked forward to the prospect that he could fill the three vacancies of these soft-on-crime judges. If so, the California Supreme Court would reclaim its reputation as one of the best in the nation.

Final result on election day? By a margin of 67% to 33% voters chose not to reconfirm Bird. Reynoso and Grodin were also ousted.

I'll explain shortly how the Willie Horton ad grew out of the Bird initiative. First, however, I must, in the interest of full disclosure, report on the dumbest thing I ever did in my twenty-seven years at the Dolphin Group.

As previously described, when we ran George Deukmejian's campaign for governor in 1982, our opponent in the

Republican primary was Mike Curb. Now, four years later, he paid us the ultimate compliment by asking us to run his campaign for lieutenant governor, a position he had held under Jerry Brown from 1979 to 1983. Bill dispatched me to handle this, and I left the Crime Victims for Court Reform campaign in the capable hands of Lee and Dolphin associate Debbie Goff, marking the first time I ever had the title "campaign manager" in a statewide race.

Although I was devoted to the Rose Bird effort, this was a pleasant change of pace. That was a very difficult and emotional campaign. And, truth be told, I always preferred working with candidates as opposed to causes.

Mike was a fun guy—just a little older than I, great sense of humor, easy to travel with. He was quite the entrepreneur. He had a movie company, record company, and racecar company (his favorite, but a big money loser). His offices were at Universal Studios, so it was fun to go over there and get on the lot.

In California, governor and lieutenant governor candidates of the same party do not run as a ticket. There was no love lost between Deukmejian and Curb thanks to their bitter primary battle four years earlier. We had to force the ticket concept by printing up bumper stickers and other campaign material that read, "Deukmejian/Curb – Team '86." We told George that if he was tapped in 1988 to run for vice president—a real possibility—he could never turn over the governor's office to Leo McCarthy, the Democrat incumbent lieutenant governor running for another term. Thus, actively supporting Mike was in his best interest.

As the election neared, Duke's coattails didn't appear long enough for us. My embarrassing moment occurred less than a week before voters went to the polls. McCarthy was running nasty attack ads against Curb, and Bill instructed everyone at Curb headquarters to do what campaigns often do: call in to a radio show on which your opponent is appearing. About five of us were on hold when my call was put through.

I'll let the *Los Angeles Times* of October 31, 1986, continue the narrative:

> *The rapidly deteriorating campaign for lieutenant governor between Democratic incumbent Leo T. McCarthy and Republican challenger Mike Curb deteriorated further Thursday when Curb's campaign manager, disguising his voice and pretending to be a member of the public, telephoned a live radio program to assail McCarthy.*
>
> *Curb's campaign manager, Fred Karger, used the name "Tony" when he called the "Michael Jackson Show" on KABC to heckle McCarthy, a guest on the show. Using a tough-sounding voice, Karger said he was "sick and tired" of McCarthy's campaign of "attack, attack, attack" against Curb and complained that the lieutenant governor's latest television ad "stinks."*
>
> *Despite trying to disguise his voice, two reporters in the studio recognized Karger almost immediately.*
>
> *"A Rich Little I'm not," said Karger later, trying to laugh off his poor impersonation of an indignant voter. A one-time actor, he said, "Now you know why I got into politics."*
>
> *Talk-show host Jackson, with his clipped British accent and gentlemanly demeanor, suspected something was fishy once "Tony" began his tirade. He interrupted Karger's harangue to say: "You know what I think, respectfully, Tony? I think you are a setup."*
>
> *"I resent that," said Karger indignantly, who claimed that he was a voter calling from his job.*

After the show, the two reporters, Linda Breakstone of the *Los Angeles Herald Examiner* and Mark Coogan of KABC-TV who both knew me well, called the office. I ducked them and called Bill. "Deny it," he said. And off he went to a meeting.

As more calls from other reporters came in to Curb headquarters, I called Lee. Having talked to Breakstone, he said, "Fred, you have to come clean. They know you. They recognized your voice."

After reading about all of my event crashing and my secret life as a gay man, you might find it hard to believe, but I am an honest person at heart. (I hope this book demonstrates that.) Here I was, under great duress, told by the head of my firm to deny something that I had done and told by another principal in the firm to tell the truth. I chose the truth and fessed up using what now seems like a feeble joke about not being a very good actor.

Although I had rejected his instructions, Bill was a prince. "Don't worry," he said. "I'll stick up for you." Then he added: "Go home. You're gone. Disappear."

Curb unwittingly kept the story alive by taking a call from the radio show at home the next day. He tried to apologize. While laying low, my worst fear came true; ABC Network News wanted to do a story on dirty tricks in campaigns that year, which would have taken the strictly California item, national. I think my inaccessibility helped kill that story.

My role in the campaign was over. I'd left with a big black mark on my record. For several days, I barely ate, couldn't sleep. It was a very rough time because the worst thing you can do is to hurt your candidate. Mike Curb, whom I so liked and admired, didn't deserve this. Adding insult to injury, Leo McCarthy himself sent me a dozen roses the day after the gaffe. Not funny.

If there's anything resembling a silver lining to this story, it's that I didn't cost Mike the election. He was far behind in the polls when I committed my ruse. I was relieved to see that he lost by a considerable margin. If it had been a down-to-the-wire loss, it could have been attributable to the call. I'd have been even more devastated.

A postscript: A friend who was a close adviser to Duke told me that the governor was indeed asked to join George H.W. Bush on the ticket in 1988. But, saddled with a Democratic lieutenant governor to whom he couldn't entrust California, Duke declined. He wasn't too happy about it.

***

Of course, Mr. Bush eventually selected Dan Quayle to run for vice president. I was in New Orleans for the 1988 convention to announce the formation of the Committee for the Presidency (CFP). Steve Garvey was to head the committee, and I was to serve as campaign director.

CFP was classified as an "Independent Expenditure Committee." Independent was the operative word. As Lee Atwater later said of us, "I would curse you by day, and pray for you at night." As part of the formal Bush/Quayle campaign, he could not have any formal contact with us; otherwise he would be violating federal election laws. He had publicly distanced himself from our actions, but privately he was apparently delighted to see what we were doing on behalf of his candidate.

Our committee was born in May of 1988 when Bill figured that it might be a good idea to get an opposition effort going against Michael Dukakis. As with other Dolphin Group start-ups, we didn't have a client. We jumped in for three reasons. First, we supported Bush. Second, we wanted to be a player for the prestige, contacts, and potential for future business. And third, if we could do commercials at some point during the campaign, we could make some money.

How do you establish such a committee? Bill, who it turned out had only weeks to live, and I compiled a list of about one hundred potential donors. Then he and I started going down the list and making calls. Here, as in similar efforts, most people don't return your calls.

One guy did. Garvey. Nicknamed "Mr. Clean," due to his spotless image, the All-Star had retired from baseball in 1987. He had been involved in Republican politics, and many observers thought he would soon run for office in California.

There was a bit of luck in enlisting Garvey. When he called me back, he said he had just been in a White House tennis tournament with Vice President Bush. Apparently he thought I was following up on behalf of Bush. I didn't disabuse him of the notion.

I told Garvey that I was going to be in San Diego the following week and would love to meet with him. He was available, so I made the two-hour drive. I asked Richard Flannery, a professional fundraiser whom I hired in the 1982 Deukmejian campaign, to join us. The three of us met at Garvey's beautiful office.

Garvey, who now headed a business management firm for professional athletes, couldn't have been nicer. He signed on. With him on board as chairman, CFP was able to attract other heavy hitters.

Barry Goldwater's adverse reaction to a limousine notwithstanding, I'd learned years earlier that you should pamper your principals. I used my connections to get Garvey on the private jet of Donald Bren, billionaire owner of the Irvine Company, who was flying from California to the convention. Lee raised some money for my expenses and I flew commercial and met him there.

Setting up interviews with Garvey was easy. Most of the political reporters were male and liked sports and were excited to meet with such a star, especially one who was rumored to be considering a run for office. The New Orleans convention served as an excellent launching pad for our fledgling committee.

Soon after we returned to California, I was able to get several prominent Republicans, including Congressman Bill Thomas of Bakersfield, to join our cause. Our real hero, however, was Susan Golding. A member of the San Diego County Board of Supervisors at the time, Susan would go on to serve as mayor of San Diego from 1992 to 2000. We had much in common. She, too, was Jewish, very moderate, and pro-choice. She had created a committee of California local elected Republican officials patterned after the GOP's national model, and I had volunteered to run it. Now she signed on as a CFP co-chair. By election day, she was far and away our best fundraiser.

The money raised went to a campaign that conjured memories of the Rose Bird effort of '86. After reading about Willie Horton in the July issue of *Reader's Digest*, we were able to track down the two families who had suffered at his hands. Donna Fournier Cuomo's 17–year-old brother Joseph had been brutally murdered by Horton in Massachusetts in 1974. Sentenced to life in prison without parole, Horton had been granted a weekend furlough in June of 1986. He had not returned. In April 1987, he had then repeatedly raped Angie Barnes after pistol whipping and stabbing her fiancé (now husband) Cliff Barnes twenty-two times.

Donna was a Republican supporting Bush. Cliff and Angie were neutral. The three, who had never met, agreed to tell their painful stories so that the public could make an informed decision in the presidential race. After the convention, I organized press conferences where they did just that. The first was in San Diego in front of a packed house. Susan Golding introduced them.

Then it was on to Los Angeles. Due to airplane problems, we were almost an hour late. The media waited, and that evening the story led all three network news broadcasts. Eventually, we crisscrossed the country.

At these emotionally charged events, Cliff and Donna did all of the talking. Angie was, understandably, uncomfortable telling her story. Obviously, no one could question their sincerity.

In Sacramento, my business partner and Dolphin Group president Carl Haglund shot two commercials one with Donna and one with Cliff. If you are of a certain age or a political junkie, you may remember photos of the menacing Horton juxtaposed with photos of Dukakis. The story of the murder and rape was then told with the finger pointing clearly at the man who was governor when Horton was furloughed. This was not our commercial. I repeat: this was not our commercial. It was done by the National Security Political Action Committee, a wholly different, unrelated independent expenditure committee. It was nasty and I don't condone it.

I'll leave it to a comprehensive study by Brown University to recap our ad:

On September 22 and following, news stories began appearing that told the tragic tale of Angie and Clifford Barnes, the woman raped and man assaulted by Horton. While on leave from a Massachusetts prison, Horton had broken into their house. According to the victims, for 12 hours, Barnes was "beaten, slashed, and terrorized" and his wife raped.

October news stories about the "Revolving Door" ad explicitly mentioned that Barnes and Cuomo, the sister of the youth murdered by Horton, were appearing on a nation-wide speaking tour that visited Illinois, Texas, California, and New York, among other states. Most of these articles did not point out that the two-million dollar tour was funded by a pro-Bush independent group known as the Committee for the Presidency. Barnes also was a guest on a number of television talk shows, such as Oprah Winfrey and Geraldo Rivera.

Shortly thereafter, a political action committee broadcast two "victim" ads featuring Barnes and Cuomo, respectively. Speaking into the camera, Barnes told the story of the rape and assault, and complained, "Mike Dukakis and Willie Horton changed our lives forever....We are worried people don't know enough about Mike Dukakis."

Cuomo meanwhile argued that "Governor Dukakis's liberal furlough experiments failed. We are all victims. First, Dukakis let killers out of prison. He also vetoed the death penalty. Willie Horton stabbed my teenage brother nineteen times. Joey died. Horton was sentenced to life without parole, but Dukakis gave him furlough. He never returned. Horton went on to rape and torture others. I worry that people here don't know enough about Dukakis's record."

These victim ads are what we produced and aired in select markets. It was the Bush/Quayle campaign's good fortune that our California press tour was just two days after Quayle's debate with the Democratic candidate for vice president, Lloyd Bentsen.

Attention moved away from Quayle's less-than-stellar performance to the moving words of Cliff and Donna.

A few days before the election, we experienced the icing on the cake. On ABC's "Nightline," anchor Ted Koppel interviewed Governor Dukakis. About ten minutes into the program, Koppel showed Dukakis our two commercials. Dukakis had stumbled in one of the presidential debates when asked how he would feel about capital punishment if his wife were raped and murdered. Now he stumbled again when confronted with the tragic stories of the Barneses and Fourniers.

I know there remains a great deal of resentment toward the Horton ads, especially the one done by the National Security PAC. Say what you want, but it was a brilliantly executed opposition campaign. There are two sides to every election. Bill Roberts used to say, "People vote *for* one guy, or *against* the other. You need to give them reasons for both."

In an opposition campaign, your goal is to provide that symbolic example that people can really relate to. You don't want to say so-and-so is too liberal or too conservative; you want to show it. (Over the last year, I have done this with Mike Huckabee, who has been guilty of the most hateful rhetoric against the gay community. As governor of Arkansas, he commuted the 108-year sentence of Maurice Clemmons, a convict who, when freed by Huckabee, murdered four police officers as they sat in a Lakewood, Washington, coffee shop.)

The Committee for the Presidency was a nice feather in the cap for the Dolphin Group after our founder and leader's death in

June. We never did get a fee for our work, but we did get a big thank you—from the White House.

Thank your supporters is a cardinal rule of politics. A few weeks before the election, I received a call from (if memory serves) Frank Lavin, President Reagan's political director. He loved what we were doing and offered to set up a post-election luncheon at the White House for CFP's major donors.

We could have anyone short of the president speak at the luncheon, Frank said. About a week after Bush's victory, I called him back. "How about Nicholas Brady?" The President-elect had already announced that he would retain Brady, the current secretary of the Treasury.

In mid-December I traveled to Washington with more than twenty of our top donors and Cliff and Angie Barnes and Donna Cuomo for a luncheon in the White House's Roosevelt Room. Susan Golding was on the list, too, but couldn't come.

At the appointed hour, I proudly presented our group as instructed at the west gate on Pennsylvania Avenue. Everyone was very excited ... until the guard looked at his clipboard and said, "I'm sorry, but the lunch has been cancelled."

"No," I said. "There must be a mistake. We're here for lunch with the secretary of the Treasury. We're all here from California."

We even had two California congressmen with us, Bill Thomas and Bill Lowery. It didn't matter. Thomas took off, so Lowery and I went into Frank Lavin's office and worked the phones in an attempt to salvage the lunch. Apparently the president and vice president were both in the West Wing. When that happens, outside visitors are not allowed.

Frank tried to help us pull a rabbit out of the hat. Secretary Brady had already changed his schedule and was no longer available. And so we ended up having lunch around the corner at the Willard Hotel with a Treasury undersecretary. Needless to say, my contingent was not happy. I'm sure they had bragged to their friends they'd be having lunch in the White House with a cabinet member. They had come all the way from California. The undersecretary, poor guy, got pummeled as most in the group were still angry. By the time we all made it to a meeting with California U.S. Senator Pete Wilson in his office, our contingent had calmed down.

A final thought on the Horton ads controversy: About four years ago, I met George H. W. Bush. During our visit, I told him I was the guy that did one of the commercials. His response went something like this: "Yeah, we got a bum rap on that. He was a bad guy."

Here I am as "The Beav" at about eight years old.

My parents Jean and Bob Karger at their home in Glencoe, IL.

Raquel Welch was having some work done on her dress backstage at the 1972 Oscars. She was about to present an award and was a little stressed, but agreed to pose for this photo.

Not too many photos like this with Mr. and Mrs. Alfred Hitchcock. This was at Jamie and Marshall Field IV's annual Beverly Hills Oscar bash at the Bistro in 1972.

Film legend Charlie Chaplin was welcomed back to Hollywood at the 1972 Academy Awards. I got to shake his hand as the show came to a close. Ann-Margret is on my arm.

This was the handshake that sealed the deal and I officially became a "Rockefeller Republican." I was lucky enough to meet Gov. Nelson Rockefeller in Chicago when he was running for President in 1968.

The first candidate whose campaigns I was really involved with and a true political hero of mine, former U.S. Senator Charles Percy (R-IL).

At the 1972 Bistro Oscar Party: Playboy founder Hugh Heffner and girlfriend Barbi Benton.

Girlfriend Barb Fine and I rode on former Vice President Hubert Humphrey's campaign plane overnight to Houston in 1972. He had just lost the Democratic nomination for President the night before to Senator George McGovern.

I met then supermodel Candice Bergen backstage at the 1973 Oscars. She had just accepted her father's honorary Academy Award.

The breakfast scene on *Owen Marshall, Counselor at Law* with my first television family—Patricia Smith, Scott Jacoby and Richard Anderson.

The closing of the Academy Awards in 1973 was very exciting. Here I am with Best Supporting Actress Eileen Heckart, Best Supporting Actor Joel Grey and Best Actress winner Liza Minnelli.

Here I am with my boss, mentor and friend, the great Bill Roberts in his office. Notice the two Air Force One flight certificates on the wall.

Drinking margaritas with legendary CBS News anchor Walter Cronkite at the 1984 Republican National Convention in Dallas.

Feeding a shrimp to *The Young and the Restless* star Brenda Dixon the night we met at a Jon Epstein party. We went on a few dates.

To Fred Karger
with best wishes Ronald Reagan

One of President Reagan's last signed photos as a result of a White House visit in December 1988.

This might be the only photo of the victims of convicted murderer Willie Horton on our Texas tour. I ran the Committee for the Presidency to help elect George H.W. Bush in 1988. *L to R:* our Co-pilot, Nicholas Thimmesch, II, Donna Fournier Cuomo, me, Susan Strader, Cliff and Angie Barnes, the Pilot and our Finance Chair and plane owner Timothy L. Strader.

I helped elect George "Duke" Deukmejian Attorney General and then Governor of California. Here's George with his wonderful wife Gloria at our headquarters opening in Manhattan Beach in 1981.

Carl Haglund (left) and Lee Stitzenberger (right), my two partners at the Dolphin Group, on our Goodyear Blimp ride to welcome new California State University Chancellor Dr. Barry Munitz.

Here I am with President and Mrs. Reagan in Los Angeles soon after he left office.

With President George H. W. Bush at an
Arnold Schwarzenegger fundraiser in
Los Angeles in 2006.

Filmmaker extraordinaire, Reed Cowan
and his partner Greg Abplanalp in
San Francisco March 2009. Reed was
just beginning to film his award
winning documentary, *8: The Mormon
Proposition.*

Fox Business Channel's Stuart Varney had me on right after Proposition 8 passed to
discuss our boycotts. He was tough, and balanced.

I organized this demonstration at Mitt Romney's book signing at the Mormon book store in San Diego. We also ran ads asking Romney to use his vast influence with his faith to get the Mormon Church to stop its vicious campaign against gay marriage.

We launched our "Don't Buy Bolthouse" boycott with a demonstration in front of Ralphs grocery store on Sunset Blvd. in Hollywood.

Our big demonstration in front of Boom Boom Room owner Steven Udvar-Hazy's AIG office in Century City. We were led by famous bagpiper Lorne Cousin.

On the first anniversary of the Manchester Hotels Boycott in San Diego, the original organizers all spoke at the rally. Here I am with Unite Here Local 30 President Bridgette Browning, Cleve Jones and Nicole Murray-Ramirez.

Seven out of twelve winners of the SAVE the BOOM!!! calendar contest at our Launch Party in Laguna Beach.

I got to meet *Daily Show* star and that night's Oscar host, Jon Stewart at the Vanity Fair Party at Morton's.

Jake Gyllenhaal was nominated for *Brokeback Mountain* in 2006 and I was there to wish him well at the Vanity Fair Party.

Cousin Dave Karger with his Grandmother and my Aunt Mimi Karger in Peterboro, New Hampshire, on my first campaign trip in February 2010.

In front of the famous Peterborough Diner in February 2010 on my first trip to New Hampshire.

This past December I came out to my mom and dad. Although they did not handle the news too well...and still to this day struggle and do not approve of it...it was the single most liberating and freeing feeling to finally come out. I became comfortable in my own skin and thought I had lived with the harassing comments and threats from them far too long.... I was done being questioned every time we would get on the phone and exhausted from hearing "if you are gay we want nothing to do with you...don't call, don't come visit" "You are disgusting." I sent my coming out letter two days before Christmas...an entire year after initially writing it. Some might say it was the coward way to do it...but it was the right way for me to approach it at the time.

After reading the "disgusting news" they asked out of respect to not come out to any other family members, friends, or anyone else back in KS because they could not imagine going to family gatherings or just to the market knowing that others are aware that their son is gay. I have given them more than enough time to digest the news and now realize this is no longer about them but about me, so I know the next step is to come out to my friends back in KS. I guess I will soon know who my real friends are and who are not.

I will one day be married to the guy of my dreams and I will be able to prove to any doubters, my parents included, that yes it is possible!

CHAPTER EIGHT

"WE NEED TO HAVE A TALK."

June 5, 1991. Lee Stitzenberger and I are meeting with a new client. Our receptionist interrupts the meeting with an urgent call for me. I go to my office to take it. On the line is the mother of my good friend, whom we'll call Rob Ellman. His parents live in Boston, but Mrs. E is calling from Rob's house here in L.A. She has not come to town for pleasure. She is here to tend to her middle son, who like so many others I know has AIDS. She says she needs me right away.

I go and tell Lee and the client that I'm very sorry but I have to leave. I don't say it's a matter of life and death, but the urgency in my voice is unmistakable.

Understandably, Lee is horrified. I know what he's thinking: *You can't just leave.* But I can ... and I must.

I rush to Rob's house in the Hollywood Hills, where his mother is caring for him. Mrs. Ellman is a stunning, petite, elegant woman in her mid-fifties. As always, she is dressed impeccably. In many ways she reminds me of my own mother. She looks so together on the outside, but she can't hide her sadness and fear.

We drive about thirty minutes to downtown Los Angeles, to a street near the Convention Center. This is not one of the city's finer neighborhoods. Mrs. Ellman takes off all her jewelry; into her purse it goes. Then we get out of the car and walk into a rundown building where she has been sent by Rob's doctor.

We find the right apartment number and knock. A small slot in the door opens. Only a pair of eyes is visible. Words are exchanged. Four hundred dollars in cash is passed through the opening, and a package of pills is passed back our way.

Safely back in the car, she thanks me. I tell her I am so happy that I can help. We drive back to Rob's house.

Mrs. Ellman gives Rob's care provider the package, the fruits of her transaction. Medicine. Illegal, black market drugs to combat the severe stomach problems that are literally starving Rob. He can't eat. He is wasting away. This new drug is believed to help, but is not yet approved for use to treat AIDS in the U.S. Her hope and mine is that these pills will delay or inhibit the ravages of the disease, postpone death.

There is no time to lose. So those with the resources like the Ellmans turn to the black market, buy the pills that have come into the U.S. from Mexico. They are directed to the sellers by doctors whose hands are tied, who don't have the drugs and can't legally prescribe them.

Watching these last several months how Mr. and Mrs. Ellman have embraced their gay son, their son dying of AIDS, and all of his friends, I begin to think of my relationship with my own parents. I am forty-one years old. And although I gave up acting professionally almost fifteen years ago, I am still acting in front of them. The Ellmans remind me of my own parents. If they can handle all this, maybe my parents can deal with having a son who is gay.

***

You may have noticed that the previous three chapters focused almost exclusively on my work. It's no accident that I didn't mention my personal life when talking about my professional life. I tried very hard to keep those two worlds separate. For example: although Lee was one of my closest friends, and although he had made some comments over the years that suggested to me that he knew I was gay and that it didn't matter, I did not give him the details of my hurried trip to help Rob. And at that point we'd been colleagues for over a decade.

Lee was and is as open to all kinds of people as anyone could be. Our friendship did not change after I started bringing my boyfriend to office events nine or ten years later. Bill Roberts was not the least bit homophobic. No one I worked closely with ever was. So why not share my secret with them as I had shared it with trusted friends? Because even if they liked me for whom I was, being openly gay was still not all that common in the 1980s and 1990s. Indeed, it still isn't. Coming out could have posed a risk with clients. And the last thing I wanted to do then was to jeopardize our business and my career.

Consider the one time I did involve myself with a gay/lesbian civil rights issue. I've already explained how risky it was for me to try and create Republican opposition to Proposition 6, the Briggs Initiative, in 1978. What I didn't mention was how that effort came back to haunt, if not threaten, me two years later.

In 1980, our client, Ray Hanzlik, a moderate Republican, was running for the U.S. Senate in California. During the primary, Ray got a letter from Carl Olson, a candidate for State Assembly and one of my detractors from the Young Republicans. It read:

"How can you have someone like this working for you who supports the homosexual agenda?"

Attached was a copy of the page showing my $100 donation to the fundraiser at which George McGovern had spoken two years earlier. Also attached were a couple of newspaper stories about the event and the role of the Young Republicans. Ray threw the material down on my desk and said, "You should know who your enemies are. This doesn't affect me one iota, but I want you to have it."

I still have the letter. This near "outing" scared the hell out of me. I realized there were consequences to my actions, or could be. And so the incident drove me further into the closet. For many years, I never gave another contribution of $100 or more to any gay-related political cause, since that's the reporting threshold.

Caution was always my middle name after that. Cardinal Rule #1: If you are a political consultant with a client running for office, you put his or her campaign bumper sticker on your car. Cardinal Rule #2: If you are a political consultant who happens to be gay, then you better park said car far away from the gay bar to which you are going.

Yes. After joining the Dolphin Group, I still frequented gay bars in West Hollywood and elsewhere, but boy was I paranoid. After parking, I walked with my back to traffic on Santa Monica Boulevard, so oncoming cars couldn't see my face. If necessary, I would cross the street to make sure I was unrecognizable. (After I was in a bar, I relaxed. I figured that if I saw another closeted person, we were both busted. It was a little like the Cold War theory of Mutual Assured Destruction; you didn't worry about the other guy outing you because you knew he'd be outing himself.)

Every so often I went to the Hay Loft, the gay bar where I had run into the ad agency exec who'd helped me get the Edge commercial. A few evenings a week the bar showed old movies in 16 mm format. On Thanksgiving eve of 1979, the James Bond classic "Goldfinger" was playing.

I'd seen the movie when it came out in 1964. Remember how the bad guys run a Lincoln Continental through a trash compactor and it comes out about the size of a suitcase? As that scene approached, I told a good looking guy in his early twenties who'd caught my eye, "Watch them wreck this brand new Lincoln." Well, it had been new when the movie came out fifteen years earlier!

Great line, eh? We started talking. His name was Geoff Walbridge, and he was a student at UCLA.

Geoff and I went out on a couple of dates and fell in love. Soon he moved in with me. With the exception of a brief breakup in 1982, we were together until Labor Day of 1990. Our relationship as a monogamous couple during the height of the AIDS crisis probably saved each of our lives.

If the good news was that we had a great love, the sad news was that we felt the need to keep it secret from family, coworkers, and all but a few friends—*for eleven years*. Geoff came from a Mormon family. His parents were divorced, and he remained close to his mother, who lived in Los Angeles. He worked with her and his stepfather in their clothing business.

Like a lot of gay people, Geoff was (had to be) a good storyteller. He managed to persuade his mother that I was a friend who traveled a lot and had asked him to house sit during my absences. When his sister Donna visited from Tennessee, she'd come with her kids and stay at our house. I would move out.

When my parents came to visit, Geoff moved out. Photographs were tucked away. Clothes were hidden. What an unbelievable and terrible way to live.

In eleven years, we never spent a Christmas together. I'd go back to Chicago every year and would have to sneak out to call him. (This was before cell phones.) Talk about being second-class citizens.

I'd be around everybody over the holidays, viewed by friends and family as the unattached guy among couples that were already married. In reality, I had my own partner - sadly in the shadows - but with a wonderful, loving home life. I just couldn't talk about it. We did the same things any couple did—get a dog, fix up the house, go to Laguna or the mountains.

I can't tell you how unpleasant many of those Christmases were. Our family would go to Lake Shore Country Club and everybody would ask, "Are you dating anyone?" When you are in the closet, you're always on edge, on guard.

At work, every time I'd do an interview with reporters while representing candidates, the same question lingered in the back of my head: *Are they going to ask me if I'm married, dating someone, gay?* You want to do everything to prevent that. Talk fast. Having come out now, I can testify what a relief it is not to live that way.

Earlier I described how a lot of gay men in the television and film industry used "beards" when they went out in public with their partners. Geoff and I often did the same thing. We were friends with a great lesbian couple, Jane and Sharon, two real beauties. The four of us would go out to dinner a lot and it appeared as if we were on a straight double date.

We sometimes confounded the valet parkers. They'd pull our cars up at the end of the evening and watch as Geoff and I would get in one car and the two girls in the other. I remember one valet saying, "Why are you letting them get away?"

Jane and I also served as beards for each other. I would go to office parties, weddings, and charity functions with her. She would come to fundraisers and office parties with me. This was all a scam to preserve our secrets. I could never bring Geoff to a political or social event.

I built up a lot of frustration and resentment during all that time of living a double life. I sure don't recommend it. It took years for me to let my secret out, and it was not a burst, but a creep. (Now, that I am so active in our fight for full equality, I am sure my decades in the closet have a lot to do with it. I've become an activist so that younger people don't have to go through what I went through.)

I'm sometimes asked if friends or co-workers or clients ever told gay jokes around me or made derogatory remarks about gays and, if so, how I reacted. I did hear a few "fag" jokes over the years, and my reaction was no reaction. Here's where my head was in those days: I took heart that people would tell such jokes in my presence; obviously I had them fooled.

No one at work ever made any derogatory remarks that I can recall, but a couple of clients did. We worked with Paul Gann, of the famous Proposition 13 Jarvis-Gann duo, to put another tax initiative on the ballot in 1980. One morning while driving him around, I had to listen to him make nasty comments about ethnic groups and gays. I bit my tongue, even when he railed about "faggots." (Ironically, he later contracted AIDS from a blood transfusion during heart surgery. At that point, he *really* went after the gay community. A very sad situation all around.)

I recall an ironic conversation with one of our major agricultural clients. At lunch with Lee and me in Sacramento, he was talking about hiring somebody and said, "He's great, but you know he's gay, and I don't think our board would go along with that."

This was funny on two levels. First of all, although the board didn't know it, they already had a gay guy working for them—me. And second, the potential hire in question was not gay. He was simply fastidious and a good dresser. (How do I know he wasn't gay? I can just tell!)

I wish that all my stories about being gay in the 1980s were simply amusing. They are not. When I was in my thirties, I read the death notices in the paper every day.

You're not supposed to do that until you're in your seventies or eighties. But during the height of the AIDS crisis, that's what you did. Friends and acquaintances were dying so quickly. As a tribute to their memory and a reminder of so many friends that I lost, I kept a list which I still have. The stories of two very close friends, David Rosenthal and Rob Ellman, bear telling here.

David was a great-looking guy with unending southern charm. He'd moved to Los Angeles from his hometown, Louisville, when he was in his early twenties. When I first met him, he was working as a bartender at Studio One. His father had two clothing stores back home, and with his best friend from Kentucky, a straight guy named Truitt Bell, David started his own upscale men's clothing store. Rosenthal Truitt opened in the early 1980s in Sunset Plaza, the very fancy part of the Sunset Strip. David and Truitt had a who's who of customers, including Nancy Reagan.

I got to know David well through a mutual friend, Greg Browne. David seemed to be living the American Dream. Self-made, successful, dating great looking guys. Eventually, there were three stores in L.A. and Orange County, and a store in Dallas across from Neiman Marcus. And then he contracted AIDS.

Like many others, David had no support network in place. He had not come out to his parents and they were halfway across the country. David's friends filled the vacuum. We would bring over food and take him out to movies. Watching him deteriorate was heart wrenching. A young, healthy, vibrant man in his thirties was ravaged by this horrific disease.

David was also representative of how AIDS affected many families. His father was ill, and his mother could not "deal" with her son's fatal disease. She left it to his friends to care for him. Greg Browne took charge and was truly remarkable.

David's mother did come through for him at the very end, but how sad it was to see so much time pass when there was so little time left. I saw too many situations in which parents cut off their dying children, wanted nothing to do with them because they were gay and ill.

Rob's situation was different. His parents were so supportive. They inspired many of us to consider coming out.

The Ellmans had a very successful family business based in Boston. Rob ran their L.A. factory. Eight years younger than I, he was larger than life, fun, handsome, a character. He always drove the hottest cars of the day—a Mercedes 450 SL and later a Porsche 911. Like me, Rob was extremely social, had grown up near a big city, and had come to California so he could enjoy a lifestyle without hometown scrutiny. At the time he got sick, I believe that he had not come out to his parents. When he finally did, he had to give them what we call "the double whammy." *I'm gay. I have AIDS.*

We'd been good friends for many years, and when Geoff and I broke up in September 1990, Rob and I made a pact to hang out more together.

Initially we did do a lot of things together. We'd go out, go to parties, talk on the phone a lot. Suddenly, however, things turned strange. Rob became distant, broke plans, said he didn't want to go out. At first he offered little explanation. Then rumors started that he might be sick. My long held policy was that I never asked. Being HIV positive was very personal, and if and when someone wanted to share that information, that was completely up to him. But I broke my own rule that one time and asked Rob at dinner one night. He told me that he was fighting AIDS and asked me to please not tell anyone.

I was devastated. Not Rob, too. Not my close friend. He showed great courage, and it brought us even closer. I told him that I would be there for him and would absolutely keep his secret.

Soon Rob started getting very sick and his mom and dad would come to care for him. They were incredible. They would fly out regularly, arrange for a caregiver/cook, get him to the best doctors ... and even purchase drugs on the black market. They not only embraced Rob, they embraced all his friends. (I remain close to them. We make a point to get together at least once a year.) Lightning struck them twice. Rob's younger brother was also gay and died of AIDS less than two years later.

Not too long after that, I was spending the day with the family in Boston. On the drive back into the city from lunch at their country club, I asked Mrs. Ellman, "Is this good? Do you like to have me around? Let me know what you would like me to do."

She said, "No, it is very important. We love having you in our lives. You're a great reminder of Rob."

Can you imagine being a parent and suffering such loss? Losing a child is the worst thing—except for losing two children this way. A lot of parents couldn't bring themselves to explain to others what had happened. There was no support network. Families were often so alone.

I took Rob out as much as I could during his last months. As with David, we usually went to "safe" places where it was unlikely they'd be seen by friends. Neither wanted people to know they had AIDS. On what may have been our last big outing, we went to a Texas-themed party in Nicholas Canyon, a lavish affair held every summer by friends of Rob.

Rob was a proud guy. He was quite sick, but he wanted to go to this party. I stood by him as he went up to say hello to people. He was so ill, they didn't recognize him. He'd say, "It's Rob," and they'd say, "Oh, I'm so sorry." It was painful to watch. You think (or at least hope) that you don't look any different on the outside.

On the night before Rob died, I was at the hospital with his parents. They pulled me out of his room and said, "Can we have Rob's memorial at your house? He loved your home and loved you."

"Of course," I said, "I'd be honored."

A month later about fifty people gathered for cocktails and to celebrate Rob's life at my place. Many stories were shared. We heard from his parents about his funeral in Boston. His father broke down. It was a tough day.

(I went to dozens of memorials and funerals like this. You'd often hear that someone who'd been fine three days earlier was in the hospital with pneumonia, and a day later he'd be dead. Our community was decimated. To this day many of us don't know what happened to certain people. We just assume they're gone if we haven't heard from them in a while.)

Having seen how beautifully Rob's parents had handled his double whammy, I knew it was time to have "the talk" with my mine. At least I could assure them that I wasn't HIV positive. (Most of us who are gay have had "the talk" with friends, if not family. You recall these episodes vividly. Each is different. All are memorable.)

By 1991, my parents had downsized to a smaller home in Glencoe. They were getting older and my mom had been battling cancer, so I visited as often as I could. Unsure exactly how they would take the news that I had put off for so many years, I didn't want to have the talk over a holiday or on the occasion of a birthday. I didn't want it to be known as "the *Christmas Fred ruined.*" So on a routine visit in the fall of 1991, I resolved to come out to them.

I arrived home on a Thursday. The next day I said, "We need to have a talk." That way I knew that I couldn't avoid it one more time. And then after breakfast on Sunday, before heading to the airport, I told them I had something to say. They both sat down on the couch in the den, and I sat in a matching chair across from them. On cue, they each lit up a cigarette.

"I'm gay," I said. Wow, that felt good!

My mother immediately started crying. My father looked slightly uncomfortable. In a deep voice, he said, "Whatever you do is fine with us." Then he went off to his office at the other end of the house.

"Have at me," I said to my mom. "Any questions?"

We then just had a good, honest conversation. For the first time in forty-one years, I finally was able to share my complete life with my mother—which is pretty great. I wish I could have revealed myself earlier. But I count myself lucky. Many people never get to have that conversation.

Were my parents surprised? My mother later told me, "Oh, I knew when you were in college." I'm not sure I buy that, but I do think she and my dad were suspicious. I'd always had girlfriends through high school and all through college, and then, for all intents and purposes, that had stopped. Still, it seemed like my mother always asked me if I were dating someone.

There was one occasion when I thought she might be on to me. Whenever my parents visited me in Los Angeles, they generously offered to take my friends out to dinner. I brought Geoff along one evening to the Hamburger Hamlet, explaining that he was a good friend.

The waitress came to the table and asked if she could get anybody a cocktail. My mother said, "Oh, no thank you." My dad, Geoff, and I ordered drinks. As the waitress started to leave, my mother said, "On second thought, I'll take a vodka on the rocks." A sign, I think she needed it to get through the dinner.

In retrospect I've come to see that all parents just want their kids to be happy. That's really the bottom line. My parents could finally see that I had nice friends and a great life and they'd been missing half of it. Coming out was a wonderful thing. I'm so glad I did it before they died.

I'm glad I told my brother, too.

My parents had asked, "Have you told Dick?"

"No. But let me be the one to tell him. Let me do it on my own terms."

Most of my gay friends came out to siblings first and then their parents. Some told one parent and asked them not to tell the other. That always amazes me. It's a pretty big secret to keep from a spouse.

About six months after I told my folks, I broke the news to Dick and his wife Christine. They already knew, even though I'd asked my parents not to say anything.

They took it very well. My brother, who is pretty conservative, not the most emotional guy in the world, said, "We love you just the same." What a nice surprise that was. Before that day, the word "love" had never creeped into his vocabulary with me.

***

After breaking up with Geoff, I was single again. While I went to my share of gay bars post-relationship, I also discovered the emerging big gay party scene. These party weekends were new in the early 1990s and came about to some extent to help us forget the horrors of AIDS that surrounded all of us. Gay men could get together for a fun weekend and let loose.

There were several cities on the party circuit, and I went to some of them: Austin, Atlanta, Miami, San Francisco, and Palm Springs, where it all began with the annual White Party. That event is held over Easter weekend each year. About 10,000 to 20,000 people, the vast majority of them gay men, attend a series of weekend parties. There's music, dancing, liquor, and drugs. Again, in the interest of full disclosure, at various times I partook of all of these. I guess my daring and curious nature took hold. No excuses. I should have just said no. Those party days are behind me now.

While fun, the party weekends occupied little of my free time in the 1990s. I decided that I wanted to get actively involved in one of the growing number of HIV/AIDS organizations in Los Angeles. After a lot of research, I decided to volunteer with Los

Angeles Shanti, a not-for-profit AIDS service organization. Now that I was no longer having to care for sick and dying friends thanks to wonderful medicines like AZT that were coming into use, I wanted to help those I didn't know. L.A. Shanti was a smaller agency where I thought that I could really make a difference. The Shanti model offered psychological counseling for HIV positive people, those who may be partnered with them, and family members.

After meeting with the executive director, I became very involved. I wanted to be a counselor, but that required a minimum of one night a week, which was difficult for me because I was doing a lot of traveling for work. Instead I became active on several committees and helped with public relations, events, and fundraising.

I've been very fortunate that I've remained HIV negative all these years when that crisis decimated my friends and my community. I saw so many friends get sick and die, and I don't presume to say I know what that feels like. But I do know what it feels like to be looked at by people who think you have AIDS.

During the several years that I was involved with L.A. Shanti—it has since closed due, thankfully, to a lack of business—I developed some precancerous growths on my face. The treatment temporarily rips your face apart and your skin becomes very red and blotchy. People with AIDS often had similar looking lesions called Kaposi's sarcoma.

During the worst period of my treatment, I went to Shanti for a meeting. People looked at me differently than before. They assumed I must be "positive." I didn't feel I could say, "Oh, I'm just having treatments." It was uncomfortable, awkward, and most of all eye-opening—a tiny glimpse of how people who actually were positive must have felt when they were (or still are) treated differently as they went about their lives.

***

I prefer to end this chapter on a lighter note—with a story about my parents. My father died in 1998 and my mother in 2003. After I came out to them, they grew to know my world and accept it and me. The first time they came to California after "the talk," I wanted them to meet some of my friends. I put together a small group one night that included Jane and Sharon, the two hot blonde lesbians. At dinner they sat on either side of my father.

As I drove my parents back to their hotel that night, my dad looked bewildered. "You mean they're *both* lesbians?" he asked.

"Yeah, Dad, both of them."

"You *sure?*"

Fred,

Thank you, first of all, for paving a way politically for the LGBT community, and what I believe to be the human race in general. Acceptance is a virtue we are required to have on this earth in order to coexist peacefully. It really does help me get through this, both socially and mentally. People like you are the best people a guy can hope to meet in his life.

I came out to my fraternity, and they are perfectly okay with the situation. My hockey team has been... quiet about their response as of yet, and I'm not showering with the team so as to not get them unnecessarily agitated. They'll get comfortable with themselves eventually, but no harm has been done.

So basically... everything that I hoped would happen has happened. There is no backlash to me whatsoever. AGR Omega will have a good name because of this, and I'm proud right now to call myself a brother there. I'm also a bisexual hockey player and happy now - something at one point in my life I was sure I would never feel.

This whole situation is liberating, and thank you for your support. I hope that maybe I'll inspire the one kid to come out to his team or fraternity. It's not as bad as you think it'll be.

P.

CHAPTER NINE

"WHAT ARE WE GOING TO DO?"

November 2005. The Boom Boom Room is in danger. A multi-billionaire businessman named Steven Udvar-Hazy has purchased the property. He plans to tear down the Boom and the adjoining inn and replace them with an upscale restaurant and boutique hotel. This is bad news. The Boom, the oldest gay bar in the western United States, has been the social and cultural hub for the Laguna Beach LGBT community for years. Tentative closing date: Labor Day, 2006.

In 1996, I bought a home in this beachfront town of about 24,000 people described by the *Los Angeles Times* as a "funky-swank Orange County community with a tradition of social tolerance." I was introduced to Laguna the first weekend I moved to L.A. and have been in love with it ever since.

The Boom sits on South Coast Highway, sixty-two miles south of Los Angeles. It is part of the 24-room Coast Inn, which was built in 1927. Originally called the Seven Seas, the island-themed bar once catered to military men. Since the 1940s, it has attracted a gay clientele. When I was younger, gay celebrities like Rock Hudson and Paul Lynde and favorites of the gay crowd like Bette Midler and Martha Raye were among the regular patrons.

The property has changed hands a few times over the ensuing years. Real estate speculators Patrick O'Loughlin and James Marchese and a silent partner bought it for $4 million in

2000. They've told the *Los Angeles Times* that they struggled to make it work as the town's demographic changed. O'Loughlin and Marchese sold the building and bar five years later for $9 million to a group of investors. That group re-sold it a few months later for $12.7 million to Udvar-Hazy, who has made a fortune in the airplane-leasing business. He has also purchased property across the street.

Fearful that a new owner might close the place, the local gay community had discussed buying the property when it went on the market most recently. But because of the hot real estate market and the building's oceanfront location, the asking price was too steep. Our hope was that no one would ever pony up that much. And if someone did, that he'd keep the Boom open. But Udvar-Hazy has told the press: "A new hotel would be quite upscale, and I'm not sure from a development point of view that it is compatible with the Boom Boom Room."

Now that he's announced his plans, I wonder if there is anything that can be done to save it. At the Dolphin Group—from which I retired in 2004—I helped design plenty of public relations campaigns. The odds are against saving the Boom, but that's not what gives me pause. As a consultant, I won a lot more battles than I lost.

What makes me think twice about getting involved is something personal. If I come out to try and save the Boom, I'll have to come out of the closet. There will be no candidate or corporation to keep the spotlight away. Media coverage will focus on the man behind the effort, Fred Karger.

Yes, over the last few years, I've been more open about my sexual orientation. Still, many former clients, friends, and acquaintances may not know I'm gay. At age fifty-five, after all these years, am I ready to go public?

***

Having counseled so many candidates and been on the stump myself in Iowa and New Hampshire over the last year and a half, I know the importance of keeping an audience's attention. I hope that you, the reader, have found my tales of national and state political races and initiatives both entertaining and instructive. I've made a concerted effort to select campaigns that were important and that influenced my philosophy and my strategy as I run for the presidency.

Bill Roberts was the magnet for the Dolphin Group's political work. After he died in 1988, we did more corporate governmental affairs than candidate consulting. One exception: my work on behalf of Brooks Firestone, who was running for lieutenant governor of California in 1998, but switched races when a Congressional seat opened up. He ended up losing that one to a far right Republican in the primary.

***

As the 1990s drew to a close, I was ready for something different. Fortunately, I was in a financial position to weigh my options. Without a family and child-related costs like college tuition, I was able to save more money than many contemporaries. Also, my father and brother had invested wisely for me. Dick and I had a talk and determined that if I scaled back to half time at

Dolphin Group, I could still live comfortably. I did that in 2000. Four years later, I retired altogether.

My plan was simple: Goof off for a year or two and then do something significant. I had no idea what that significant thing would be. I just knew that I still had something to contribute and didn't want to be a dilettante for the rest of my life. Doing something to help kids along the lines of my involvement with Big Brothers was a possibility. Perhaps I'd become a mentor or volunteer with the Boys Clubs/Girls Clubs.

The goofing off part was pretty easy. Always on the go, I would take a nice trip at least once a month. I went to Europe and to South America frequently, as my close friend, Russell Johnson, had moved to Buenos Aires. New York City is such a favorite, I considered getting an apartment there. I didn't, but I'd go there three or four times a year for a week or more each trip.

My spring visit to New York coincided with the annual dinner of a gay civil rights organization, Lambda Legal. In the fall, I went to the annual meeting of the Clinton Global Initiative, which I would cover for a blog I had started. Washington, D.C., was also on my itinerary. There, each year, I'd attend the fall dinner of the Human Rights Campaign (HRC), the largest national LGBTQ political organization.

I was still not out to the world at large. What does that mean? For purposes here, let's say I was never identified in the media as gay or as a gay activist.

I had come close to doing so. In 2000, at the urging of a good friend, Brian Bennett, I had become involved with the Republican Unity Coalition (RUC). This was a gay-straight alliance of influential Republicans that a close friend of the Bush family, Charles Francis, founded to support George W. for president. As you may remember, Candidate Bush was quite different in many ways. After clinching the nomination he met with a dozen gay Republicans in the Governor's Mansion in Austin. Following the meeting he actually held a press conference on the front steps of the mansion with the group, who became known as the "Austin 12," behind him and pronounced himself a better man for the experience.

Aligning myself with an organization like RUC was the closest I had come to coming out. I even put my name on an event invitation—a big step for me. But I still had some cover. RUC's board and the list of inviters was composed of both gay and straight Republicans.

Maintaining my cover remained important. Brian was a lot braver. He was one of only three subjects of "Family Fundamentals," an incredible documentary film focusing on gays and lesbians who had come out. His was a fascinating story, as he had been the chief of staff and campaign manager for Bob Dornan, the conservative California congressman who was one of the harshest critics of gay rights. He had lived with the Dornan family for six years, but when he came out in 1997, the congressman ended their long friendship.

When the film premiered at the Sundance Festival in 2002, Mike Gillaspie, my boyfriend at the time, and I met Brian and his boyfriend Rick in Park City, Utah. Brian had invited Jean Pasco, a political reporter with the *Los Angeles Times* Orange County bureau to come along. She was writing a story about Brian, whose film was one of the big documentaries at Sundance that year.

I knew Jean from Steve Horn's congressional campaign in 1988 and had worked with her on other campaigns and projects since. I panicked when I heard she was coming. After spending time with her, I got up my nerve and asked her to please not mention me by name in her story. She was wonderful and assured me she would honor my request.

(At the Dolphin Group, I never really had "the talk" with Lee—although he frequently made remarks that suggested he was aware of my orientation and that it made absolutely no difference to him as a business partner or friend. I did come out to another close friend from work, Kathy Lucker, on a drive back from San Diego. At age twenty-two, she had started as our receptionist and office manager, and had moved up to vice president with an office right next to mine. She told me she had it all figured out many years earlier.)

***

Traveling across the country and around the world during that first year of retirement, I was content. Determined to tune out politics, I even cancelled my subscription to Dick Rosengarten's *California Political Week* (*Calpeek*), the non-partisan bulletin that junkies turn to every Friday for political news and gossip. As year two began, however, I became a little restless, missed the fray. There's just so much travel, shopping, and dating you can do. I was ready to tackle something.

Then...BOOM. Literally. After the Boom Boom Room was sold and Mr. Udvar-Hazy announced plans to close it, I looked at my friends and said, "What are we going to do?" They looked at me as if I were crazy, and reminded me that Udvar-Hazy was worth $3.1 billion. This was a Goliath that even David couldn't beat.

There was another establishment down the street from the Boom whose clientele was also primarily gay. Woody's was more restaurant/bar than bar/club. We all figured we'd just have to be content to go there once the Boom was shuttered and torn down. Then Woody's was sold and turned into a family restaurant serving Mexican food, El Ranchito.

A few months after the sale of the Boom, I was on the road again. Over the Christmas and New Year holiday, my friend Shane Miller and I went to South America—Brazil, Argentina, Uruguay, and, finally, Machu Picchu, the fifteenth-century Inca site in Peru. The lodge we stayed in afforded us access to the ruins after the day's tourists departed.

Surprisingly, no one else hiked into the deserted park for the last hour it was open. I found myself alone in a spot I had staked out earlier in the day because it had the most spectacular view. It was a warm evening and the sun was low in the sky. I was alone with my thoughts.

This was a truly spiritual moment. Electric. I can't explain it other than to say that I looked into my heart and realized I had to do something *now*. To be sure, the impulse had been building. But there, in that magnificent setting 8000 feet high, it became more urgent. I'm not saying that I had a grand notion to save the world (or run for president). I'd be content with something far smaller, but meaningful—trying to save the historic bar that meant so much to my community and preserve it and the gay life in Laguna along with it for future generations.

We don't have a lot of landmarks in the gay civil rights movement. Our clubs and our bars have long been our gathering places. They take on a far greater significance. And nothing was more significant in gay history than the Boom.

In twenty-seven years at the Dolphin Group, I learned that you have to conduct research before you can develop a plan. Home from South America, I started doing what we in the political world call due diligence.

One. Identify the players: Udvar-Hazy, of course; the mayor and city council; the planning commission; design review board; community activists; prominent citizens; the general public and the press.

I knew hardly anything about the city and its leaders. I needed to talk to lots of people to develop a strategy. I looked at campaign finance reports to see who was active in town. I attended city council meetings to see how members interacted. I needed to become an expert in Laguna Beach politics quickly.

Two. Develop a plan: Come up with a theme and a committee name. Determine various action steps. And get a website up.

By the end of March 2006, I had probably talked to fifty community leaders, including Mr. Udvar-Hazy. I didn't expect to hear back from him. He's a busy man—and was then the eighty-third richest American according to *Forbes*. But call he did.

He was very nice. I asked his specific plans and he told me that he wanted to create a boutique hotel with a five star restaurant and bar. He also planned to develop the property across the street into a mini-shopping center with art galleries and restaurants. Finally, he planned to tear down an oceanfront home and build a new one.

My next question was simple: "Would you consider keeping the new bar as a gay establishment?" If so, I continued, the gay community would work with him to get his plan approved.

"No," he said.

"You know, this is a very difficult town to get stuff done in," I said. "It took the Montage [a luxury resort], seven years to get its plans approved."

"Longer," Udvar-Hazy said.

He'd done his homework. He knew what he was up against with the City of Laguna Beach. But, while it might take time to get his plans approved, he could shut down the bar immediately if he wanted to. The only real power I had was to develop a groundswell of opposition to his project, and then maybe we could work out a compromise.

He suggested I talk with O'Loughlin, whom he had retained as the bar's manager. I called Patrick right away and suggested that we meet. It didn't happen immediately.

Meanwhile, back in full Dolphin Group mode, I would meet with as many current and former elected and appointed officials and other movers and shakers as I could. We'd have breakfast, lunch, coffee, or dinner. I would often treat, since whoever I was meeting with was helping me to learn more about what makes Laguna tick. I would always ask, "Who else should I talk to?" Then, I followed up.

Until this campaign, what I loved about Laguna was that I could tune out work. For years I'd been anonymous in town. Now I did a "180" —meeting everyone, joining everything (including the Chamber of Commerce), supporting many local organizations.

The lesson here is: if you are going to be a community organizer, become part of the community.

From the beginning there was one person I wanted in my corner more than anyone: former Laguna Beach Mayor Bob Gentry, the first openly gay person to serve as mayor of a city in the United States. He'd served on the city council from 1982 to 1994, and now split his time between the California town of Rancho Mirage and Hawaii. I had never met him, but he had always been one of my true heroes in politics—a guy who had the guts to be completely out in 1982. I would read about him in the *Los Angeles Times*, in absolute amazement. Here was an openly gay man as mayor of the city I loved, in the middle of Orange County. I was in awe of him and all he did beginning twenty-five years earlier. What an inspiration!

Bob is a very liberal Democrat, and Laguna is a pretty progressive place. Still, it's Orange County. Republicans, albeit moderate ones, held the majority on the city council now. So before asking Bob to be involved with the Save the Boom campaign, I talked to a lot of people, liberal and conservative, gay and straight, to get their thoughts on Bob. Everyone I spoke to revered him, even those who were political polar opposites. That was more than enough for me.

During our first phone conversation, Bob wished me well, but said he wasn't interested in helping. Okay, I said, I'd just keep him in the loop by sending him updates. I sent him a lot of emails over the next several months with news of all we were doing in Laguna. I planned to court him until I won him over.

And eventually, I did. The next time I called, I fibbed that it just so happened that I was going to be in Palm Springs and would love to meet him. He suggested we have coffee.

I drove down the next week loaded for bear. I had a pitch lined up and a stash of material for him. Seated outside at a Starbucks in Cathedral City, I began, "I really need your help on this."

"Okay," he said.

Enlisting him was that easy. I was stunned. Once he signed on, his insights were always helpful. He told me that some people—including city council members themselves—might suggest that the council didn't have the power to block the development plans. But that was bull, he said.

Our time together was life-altering for me for another reason. Here I was, fifty-six years old, deeply in the closet for my whole life. What was it going to be like, I asked, if/when I came out in the course of this campaign?

Bob gave me "the pep talk" (not to be confused with "the talk"). I don't remember the exact words, but he said something like, "Look, you're doing the right thing. Don't worry about it. If people don't like it, it's their problem, not yours."

From that day forward, I made no effort to hide my orientation. It had taken a long time, too long, but it finally was out there. I felt so much better. "Freeing" is the best word to describe the feeling.

Having Bob as my mentor, guide, strategist, and inspiration made a huge difference. He made it clear that I could lean on him.

I was now out, really out. By the time the Dolphin Group's annual Christmas party rolled around in 2006, I had received an enormous amount of press coverage, including several big stories in the *Los Angeles Times*. As I mingled, I was uncomfortable at first. But that was *my* problem. I found out that nobody at the party gave a damn whether I was gay or straight. It wasn't a topic of conversation. No one stayed away from me or patronized me.

Few people even brought the subject up. Karen Spencer, Stu's wonderful daughter, was an exception. After an article about me appeared in the *Sacramento Bee*, she sent me a message on Facebook: "You could have told *me*." She was right. I could have told her and most everyone else instead of waiting and enduring all the trauma (much of it self-inflicted) until I was fifty-six.

In addition to courting Bob, I did several other things to keep the bar open. By mid-April, I had a website up, SavetheBoom.com, created by my good friend Leif Strickland. He did an incredible job; we had a slick logo and a fair amount of content. Translation: we looked professional, serious, and funded.

There was a huge lesson here. I had seriously considered announcing that we were going to raise $100,000 for the effort. My reasoning? A war chest of that size would give us credibility. But oddly enough, the website itself gave us gravitas. Raising the big bucks did not have to be a priority. Thank you, Leif!

Perhaps most important, the website gave the appearance that we were an organization/movement, not a one-man band. No one knew I was doing this by myself initially. This is called "smoke and mirrors." You always want a campaign to look bigger than it is.

When Bob Gentry came on board, our credibility and the interest of the press grew tremendously. Laguna Beach is unique because it has three local newspapers; one is owned by the *Los Angeles Times,* one is owned by the *Orange County Register*, and one is owned locally. They're well read, and it's a good bet you'll get coverage when you combine the story of the re-emergence of the former mayor with the David and Goliath story about a multi-billionaire closing the last gay bar. After Bob signed on as co-chair of Save the Boom, he wrote an open letter to the community:

> *Scores of gay men and women have helped to define Laguna Beach as an art colony, a seaside resort, a charming old-world village, an open and affirming culture. It is now time for the community to come together again and save an important symbol, The Boom Boom Room and the historic Coast Inn.*
>
> *By expressing the community's value in saving this important historical business and structure, the community is affirming its respect for and tie to the gay community. Nothing could be more important at this point in time.*
>
> *Yes, this is private property and a private business. But it has the symbolism so important to the definition of Laguna Beach. Expressing one's desire to save this symbol sends a powerful message to our elected and appointed officials.*

Of course, we posted that on the website. And we also posted testimonials and remembrances from ordinary citizens:

Thank you, Fred! The Boom has been my home away from home since January 1973. I had recently returned from Vietnam and was terrified at that time, all the time, inside. The home culture had changed and I was gay, a Viet vet and there was no place for me anywhere.

I remember well that cold and rainy night I wandered in. I immediately felt warm as if I was with an old friend. The juke box was playing "He's So Vain," then "Tangerine and Green Eyes" from the '40's, then a song by WAR. I realized that for the first time in my life I felt safe. A haven. There were pool tables in what is now the dance area and goldfish swimming under the glass on the bar. The guys all seemed to know one another and with their flannel shirts and Levi's were friendly, handsome and sexy.

I have never found anything quite like the Boom.

The people I have met there were not only from Laguna, but from big cities and small towns all over the world. I fell in love in the Boom in the '70s and it changed my life. I fell in love again there in the '80s during the time of AIDS and again it changed my life. I became an activist. We all did. I have never had as much fun, or learned as much, or had so many dreams come true, or my growth as a man as I have experienced in that sweet, fine place.

Smoke and mirrors can only take you so far. There was an "action" element to my plan, too. Recent events in Provincetown, a gay-friendly haven on the tip of Massachusetts's Cape Cod, inspired another prong of our effort. There, residents had mounted a successful petition drive to stave off the sale and closure of The Boatslip. A developer had wanted to turn this longtime gay resort and bar into condominiums. I called the guy who had orchestrated that effort. He told me what he'd done and sent me a copy of the petition he had used.

Memorial Day weekend marks the kickoff of the summer season in Laguna Beach. I decided to make it the launch date of the Save the Boom campaign as well. Jeff Delancy was hired and put in charge of gathering 5,000 signatures on our petition. We brought on several more young, enthusiastic helpers over the summer, to set up tables outside supermarkets, go to the beaches, the farmers' market, the various art and entertainment venues around town, and in front of the Boom Boom Room itself. Again, we sought to look like a serious, well-funded, grassroots movement that was everywhere.

Jeff would eventually spend the summer months helping me. He stayed in one of the downstairs bedrooms, and my home was the headquarters of the effort from beginning to end. Smoke and mirrors reminiscent of a wonderful scene in a "Seinfeld" episode in which Cosmo Kramer enlists Darren, an intern from NYU, to help him launch a venture called Kramerica. When a university dean gets wind of it, she calls Kramer on the carpet:

Dean Jones: I've been reviewing Darren's internship journal. Doing laundry...

Kramer: ...Yeah.

Dean Jones: ...Mending chicken wire, high-tea with a Mr. Newman.

Kramer: I know it sounds pretty glamorous, but it's business as usual at Kramerica.

Dean Jones: As far as I can tell your entire enterprise is nothing more than a solitary man with a messy apartment which may or may not contain a chicken.

Kramer: And with Darren's help, we'll get that chicken.

In truth, my house wasn't messy, and there was a lot more to our effort. Flanked by a big banner and wearing printed yellow

T-shirts reading "SAVE THE BOOM," our Memorial Day weekend volunteers found everyone they met to be friendly, intrigued, and, very often, willing to sign. They often shared Boom stories, and many petition signers were genuinely sad at the prospect of it closing. I was surprised how many people in town had a personal connection with a gay bar. Over this weekend and a July 4 signature drive, there was only one incident in which someone hurled a homophobic slur.

(The slur, the positive remarks, and much of the campaign were captured by John Keitel, a brilliant filmmaker who has stayed on with me to chronicle my bid for the presidency. A ten-minute preview of his documentary, "Saving the Boom," can be viewed at www.savetheboom.com.)

When we began, I announced that we intended to collect 5000 signatures over the summer months—a huge number equal to about 20% of the town's population. Thanks in large part to Jeff, we collected nearly 6000 signatures in three months! We eventually brought a wheelbarrow full of the petitions into a city council meeting. The council couldn't have been more supportive. Its response was extremely helpful in the court of public opinion.

The petition drive resulted in more coverage. I continued to talk with Udvar-Hazy's man, Patrick O'Loughlin. My hope was that he would, at the very least, agree to keep the Boom open until the plans for the new hotel and restaurant were approved. Why not? The Boom appeared to be a nice moneymaker, a cash-only operation with plenty of patrons.

Patrick suggested that business was down, but you would never know it. I would often see him take a stack of twenties from the cash register and put them right into the ATM. The place was literally a "cash cow." Wouldn't it be better to generate revenue for a while instead of letting the bar sit vacant? That argument might resonate with your typical developer, but Udvar-Hazy had so much money, I imagine the revenue lost if he were to close the Boom was insubstantial.

While on a Mediterranean cruise that summer with Leif, I received word from Patrick that we'd won a one-year reprieve: the Boom's much anticipated closure would not happen as expected on Labor Day 2006. Why did Udvar-Hazy do this? My guess was that the architect he had hired and others who were counseling him told him that he could generate good will in the community and with the city council and there was little downside.

The announcement did win Udvar-Hazy some points in town, and, in all modesty, it made me a local hero—the guy who saved the Boom. In fact, I knew that the Boom hadn't been saved. Its execution had been delayed, but more work was needed to keep it open. At least now I had more time to do it.

Over the next year, I gave it my best shot. I worked on Udvar-Hazy. I worked on his architect Morris Skenderian. I worked on the city council. I even worked on Brad Pitt and George Clooney.

What roles did these superstars play? Early in 2007, Udvar-Hazy called me and threatened to sue me because a newspaper had reported that gays would not be welcomed in his planned establishment. I apologized profusely, but told him that I had never made that comment. I then asked if he would consider selling the building if I came up with a buyer. "Sure," he said.

Unbelievable, I thought. My plan had worked; I had worn him down.

Find a buyer and we save the Boom. Wow. Earlier I had approached David Cooley, who had founded the most successful gay bar in Los Angeles, The Abbey. He had sold the bar recently to SBE, a Los Angeles-based luxury hospitality, real estate development, and lifestyle company founded by Sam Nazarian, but was still running it.

David and SBE were rumored to be thinking of expanding the Abbey brand to several cities, including Laguna Beach. This might be a perfect fit. There was definite interest, but after a year of trying to broker a deal, nothing ever materialized.

It wasn't even Udvar-Hazy's fault. He continued to be reasonable. Later in the spring he called me to say he had a buyer from Texas, but if I could find a gay buyer quickly....

I couldn't, and in the process, a realtor whom I had engaged to find a buyer leaked the story to the press with my help that the property was for sale. Udvar-Hazy was furious.

The deal with the Texan apparently fell through. But now I knew that he was actually willing to sell. Enter Pitt and Clooney. I didn't pick their names out of thin air. After Udvar-Hazy had originally purchased the property in 2005, the *Orange County Business Journal* ran a story they picked from *E! Online*, that the two actors were part of a new ownership group to build the hotel and restaurant.

It never seemed plausible to me; this was a pretty small purchase. The duo had previously partnered on a massive Las Vegas condo/casino development. Udvar-Hazy had so much money that he didn't need partners. The actors denied the story, but whenever the Boom sale would come up, so did their names. So I decided to capitalize on the continuing rumor.

The Pitt/Clooney movie "Oceans 13" was premiering in Los Angeles and then Las Vegas during the first week of June 2007. Taking advantage of that buzz, I composed an ad in which I implored the actors to save the Boom. I paid $1600 to run a quarter page in *Daily Variety*, the show business bible. This was far and away my greatest expense during the entire campaign to save the bar; we really did run on a shoestring.

I have known Harvey Levin, the founder of TMZ.com, the premier site for entertainment news and gossip, for over thirty years. Prior to the ad's debut, I called him about it and gave him the exclusive. Serendipitously, the story ran on the same day that celebrity Paris Hilton was released from jail. As a result, the site (and, thus, our ad) received an unusually large amount of traffic.

TMZ came up with a great headline and did such a terrific job with the story; I'm reprinting it here in its entirety:

PITT AND CLOONEY MIXED UP IN GAY BAR FIGHT

Known for their goodwill efforts in poverty-ravaged parts of the world like Darfur, Brad Pitt and George Clooney are now being asked to come to the aid of a slightly less disenfranchised group -- Laguna Beach gays!

The Boom Boom Room, a popular Laguna Beach, Calif. gay bar for over 60 years, was sold to a Beverly Hills billionaire two years ago for over $12 million. That's a lot of cosmos!

In 2005, Pitt & Clooney were incorrectly labeled as co-investors in the bar, whose rightful owners were planning on turning into yet another upscale (and undoubtedly hetero) oceanfront hotel. The Heche Hilton! With those plans now scrapped, the bar (which is scheduled to stay open until Labor Day) is back on the market and a grassroots organization is appealing to the Hollywood hunks to help **Save the Boom***!*

C'mon guys, you know you want to! To make sure they get the message, TMZ has exclusively obtained the ad Save the Boom is running in Monday's Variety, which hopes to persuade Brad and George to "buy our 60-year-old landmark before it is converted into a boutique hotel."

And homophobes say gays are the ones doing all the converting?! If the "Oceans 13" stars decide to purchase the bar and keep the same clientele, they'll find out the only thing easier to get at The Boom than a drink is ... a phone number!

Remember, I was born with the chutzpah gene. In conjunction with the ad, we staged a peaceful demonstration when the movie premiered at Grauman's Chinese Theater in Hollywood. Then Save the Boom treasurer Shane Miller and I went to the Vegas premier the next night with the hope of talking to the actors. Unfortunately, security was on to us. They kicked us out of the area where the press waits for the stars to arrive.

I'd bought two tickets to the premiere. Those tickets guaranteed entry to the after-party, but I knew the cast would be elsewhere—a VIP party. After three failed forays, I was able to talk my way into that.

I had a Save the Boom shirt tucked into my pants. My plan was to give it to another star of the movie, Matt Damon. If he could model it and we could get a photo, it would be seen worldwide.

Damon had already left. But wait! There was Clooney. I walked towards him ... and he ran.

Bottom line: good publicity, but no new buyers. Time was running out.

And it did run out three months later. The Boom closed its doors after Labor Day weekend 2007.

It was a very emotional night that began after a nice day at the beach, with an urgent call from a friend to come to the Boom ASAP. There were already two L.A. television stations there to cover the closing night. I hopped on my scooter and hustled over.

Eight hours later, at 2 a.m., the Boom closed for the final time. There were so many people there that night to pay their respects to this remarkable little bar in Laguna Beach. It was a fun night, but as the champagne came out around 1:30, it hit all of us that this great run was over. A whole group of friends and I hit the dance floor for the last dance of the night, which was appropriately Donna Summers's song by the same name.

John Keitel was there the entire night filming for his documentary. He recorded the night and all of the fun and emotions that were a part of it. We made the evening news on four L.A. TV stations; two even did live remotes. Not too common for the closing of a bar, let alone a gay one.

Although the doors to the Boom closed, the doors to the Save the Boom effort did not. It becomes far more difficult to save a bar after it has closed, but Udvar-Hazy was still looking to sell, so I kept looking for someone to buy. The city would still have to approve any plans for the property, so I kept at it. At a charity auction, I had bid on and won the services of an architect. I commissioned him to design a plan for a complex that could incorporate the Boom. Now I showed those plans to the powers that be.

In January 2008, we launched another initiative, "Operation Post Card." Here's a portion of the press release:

SAVE the BOOM!!! today kicked off its 2008 offensive to save the landmark Coast Inn and Boom Boom Room. A winter long campaign gets underway today to appeal to Mr. Steven Udvar-Hazy to either sell his property to a buyer who will keep it as a gay establishment, donate it to the city of Laguna Beach or donate it to a newly created Trust that will administer the property.

"Thousands of yellow post cards have been printed and we hope to fill his Los Angeles office with them. We will be getting as many people to sign and mail them to Mr. Udvar-Hazy as we can until this historic property returns to the way it has been for over 60 years," stated Fred Karger, Founder of SAVE the BOOM!!!

"Mr. Udvar-Hazy is a very generous man. He donated nearly $70 million to the Smithsonian to create The Steven F. Udvar-Hazy Center of The National Air and Space Museum.... Now we sincerely hope that he will consider donating the historic building that he owns in Laguna Beach.

"The donation ... could be an excellent federal and state tax deduction for him. He would be a hero to millions of gays and lesbians across the country who support our cause," said Karger. "Real estate values are down in Orange County from what they were 2 years ago when he bought the property, and financing is hard to come by. We hope that he will either drastically lower the asking price or be a true hero and donate the property."

My plan was to wear down Udvar-Hazy so much that he would just say, "Screw this. I'm selling this thing for a penny." We generated over 1,500 postcards, but no sale.

Next strategy? Years earlier, Udvar-Hazy had sold his aircraft leasing business to a gigantic (but in January 2008, little known) company called AIG. He still ran his old business, a division of AIG, but reported to Martin Sullivan, AIG's CEO.

The Human Rights Campaign publishes a Corporate Equality Index. AIG, the world's largest insurer, had a terrible track record when it came to gay civil rights. At the time, its rating was 30 on a scale of 100—right down there with the bottom feeders. People who worked there even said: *It's awful. You don't dare come out. It's homophobic.*

My plan? An LGBT boycott of AIG. First step: stage a lunchtime demonstration at its Century City headquarters. Suggest that one way to rehabilitate its image would be to buy the Boom or persuade Udvar-Hazy to save the bar.

I wrote a letter to Mr. Sullivan and received a response the next day. His representative reminded me that the Boom Boom Room investment was privately held by Mr. Udvar-Hazy and that I would have to take up the matter with him. Soon the boycott idea became moot. AIG fell apart during the Great Recession. There was no way they could buy the bar while they were getting bailout money from the U.S. government.

So where do things stand today? The city council and the Laguna Beach Design Review Board have approved major renovation plans, but Udvar-Hazy, who still owns the property, has yet to break ground. The council required him to have a wine bar as part of his new hotel, but his architect has said that Udvar-Hazy will not agree to that. The Coast Inn remains open as a fleabag apartment house, but the Boom is still closed.

The plans have been challenged. In August 2010, my good friend and political powerhouse Audrey Prosser appealed the entire project to the California Coastal Commission because it violates the city's Local Coastal Plan and conflicts with the state's goal of providing affordable visitor services along the coast. Her appeal was joined by commission staff and two commissioners, chair Sara Wan and Mary Shallenberger. The California Coastal Commission is known as the death knell for coastal development.

There is still a question as to whether or not there will be a bar or some other retail establishment as a part of a new hotel. In July 2010, the *Laguna Beach Independent* quoted project architect Morris Skenderian: "The client [Udvar-Hazy] has no interest in a restaurant or bar of any size, especially ... primarily as a gathering place for the gay community." Apparently noise and cost were the primary concerns. It was also reported that the new complex would include an "interpretive center" about the building's gay history. A tip of the hat, but an unsatisfactory one.

I should note that Audrey had managed to persuade the city and Udvar-Hazy to open the Boom for a few months in 2008. The bar was transformed into Democratic Party headquarters and the No on Proposition 8 office for the November election. There was a Halloween party—a No on 8 fundraiser—that brought back great memories of the Boom.

I spent that election night at the old Boom. But I must confess I wasn't thinking about the future of the bar. Instead, I was focused on the Proposition 8 voting. Would the state's approval of gay marriage survive the evening?

Fred,

Congratulations on your bigot-busting. You're the first Republican to take on that homophobic party, and it takes a lotta guts on your part. I admire you for your toughness.

Whether you win or not, the status quo will never be the same for them. Thank you for your willingness to stand up for those of us who did/do not fit into the heterosexual mode designed for us by our world leaders, I believe it is too messy for them to deal with those of us who cannot be easily labeled and put in a box.

Sincere best wishes in your fight against bigotry and NOM, that despicable group from Utah.

John V.

CHAPTER TEN

"I'M ON YOUR SIDE NOW."

February 11, 2009. If I didn't previously realize that I was in hostile territory, I do now. The hotel tells me it has assigned an armed security guard to stem any trouble that might arise at my press conference.

I am in Salt Lake City, Utah, on this blustery winter day. The Mormon Church is headquartered here. I've already filed complaints against the church for violating California election laws during the battle over Proposition 8. Now I'm about to announce the creation of a website (mormongate.com) to ask for the public's help in further exposing the Mormons' shameful and secretive role in funding the initiative that banned gay marriage in my state. The organization I created in 2008, Californians Against Hate, is also launching a boycott—our fourth—against a business run by one of Utah's richest, most prominent families.

You might think that all the newspapers and television and radio stations in Salt Lake City are fair and impartial. But the Mormon Church owns several of these media outlets. I'm aware that this particular sub-section might well be hostile.

I've arranged and attended more press conferences than I can count, but this is the first one where I've been the principal speaker. I have prepared bar charts, posters, and press kits. My friend Andrew Rhoda attends the press conference to welcome reporters and hand out the press kits. We look professional, and we've got an important story to tell. Still, I couldn't be more nervous.

That nervousness continues throughout my hour-long Q & A with the media. As a comedian might say, "Tough crowd."

Yet by the time it's over, something most surprising has occurred. I've been invited to a meeting in the lion's den.

***

Although the effort to save the Boom didn't change Steven Udvar-Hazy's mind, it was life-altering for me. I'd emerged from the closet. Not one person I cared about turned away from me, and I could look myself in the mirror a lot more easily. Liberated now, I was ready for a new challenge.

That challenge presented itself in April of 2008, when I attended my first national Log Cabin Republican (LCR) Convention in San Diego. At the time, a well-orchestrated drive was underway to enact a constitutional amendment banning gay marriage in California. That drive had been initiated while the legality of gay marriage was being considered by the California Supreme Court. Hundreds of thousands of signatures had already been collected to put the question on the November ballot. Ugh. Shades of the Briggs Initiative in 1978, this would eventually become the infamous Proposition 8.

Governor Arnold Schwarzenegger had previously vetoed two bills allowing gay marriage, wanting to leave it to the courts to decide. But when, at the convention, he was asked by LCR president Patrick Sammon about the potential ballot initiative (and reminded of the gay-friendly role Ronald Reagan had played with Briggs), the governor said he would "always be there to fight against [the initiative]." The press reported that this was the first time Schwarzenegger had taken a position on an initiative still being circulated.

Republican Schwarzenegger's gutsy response was the good news. The bad news was that those collecting the signatures were already frighteningly well-funded. While the convention was in session, the *San Diego Union Tribune* ran a story identifying several businessmen from San Diego as major contributors. Among the heaviest hitters were Doug Manchester, owner of the local Manchester Grand Hyatt Hotel and the Grand del Mar Hotel, and Terry Caster, owner of A-1 Self Storage. Both professed strong Catholic beliefs.

The story noted that a gay man from San Diego, Keith Gran, had suggested boycotting these mega-donors. "Why should we spend our money with these businesses, only to have it used against us?" he asked. Made perfect sense to me, and having contemplated boycotting AIG a few months earlier, I liked the idea. It was time for me to jump into this fray—not as Fred Karger, one individual, but as the face of a new group I would create, Californians Against Hate (CAH).

When CAH was born (it was renamed Rights Equals Rights in July 2010), it consisted only of myself and a few dedicated friends. Through the Internet, the potent gay blogosphere, and media, however, we have since been able to rally thousands.

On May 15, as I was in the midst of my due diligence researching Manchester and Caster and the other San Diego donors, the California Supreme Court affirmed the right to same sex marriage by a four-three decision. This surprise ruling intensified the resolve of our opponents, who by this time had 1.2 million signatures—more than enough to get their constitutional amendment on the ballot.

Although San Diego has its share of evangelical mega-churches, most of its Republicans are moderate. Many were embarrassed to learn that some big funders of the ballot initiative were their neighbors. I began to visit the city regularly to talk with the LGBTQ leadership about organizing a boycott. Manchester, who had given $125,000, seemed a better first target than Caster, even though he and his family had given $283,000 at that point. Hotels depend on conventions and meetings organized by associations and the like. Such groups are easier to reach and more likely to listen than the individuals who patronize self-storage facilities. And I had known for years that Doug Manchester was a very unpopular figure. He was the Donald Trump of San Diego, the biggest developer in the city, its biggest bully, and even named his hotels after himself a la Trump.

The gay leaders in San Diego had taken up the idea of a boycott before I arrived on the scene, and after much discussion had decided against it. They instead wanted to raise money to launch a positive campaign to defeat Proposition 8, one that featured loving same sex couples talking about why a "yes" vote on Proposition 8 would be so devastating. "Great idea," I said. "But I'm still going to do this." I wanted to kick off Californians Against Hate with a demonstration in front of the Manchester Grand Hyatt and the announcement of the boycott. Then I would leave town to work on that and other potential boycotts and actions against other mega-donors to Yes on 8.

The LGBT community in San Diego viewed me as an outsider and was dead set against the boycott. I don't blame them. They didn't know me, and if you don't live in San Diego, you are an outsider, even if you're next door in Orange County. I had experienced that San Diego way of thinking since 1978 when I was working for George Deukmejian. It doesn't matter if someone has only lived in San Diego for six months, and you have been working there for thirty years ... *outsider*. So I was well aware of what I was getting myself into.

I believe that one of the biggest LGBTQ leaders in San Diego accidentally gave me the most useful advice: approach UNITE HERE Local 30, the hotel workers union that was considering a Manchester Grand Hyatt boycott as well. I made the call as soon as I got the tip. Two days later I was having lunch with Bridget Browning, the president of the union, and Dan Rottenstreich, its political director, at the little coffee shop adjoining city hall. Quickly, we saw that we had a lot in common— and we instantly agreed to work together.

I wanted to schedule the demonstration and boycott announcement for San Diego's Gay Pride Weekend in mid-July. Again, there was major resistance from the LGBTQ establishment. Thanks to one Cleve Jones, however, we worked out a compromise.

Cleve Jones. His name may not be familiar to all readers, but he is a legend. A former intern to Harvey Milk, he founded the San Francisco AIDS Foundation in 1983; was prominently featured in Randy Shilts' groundbreaking book *And the Band Played On,* conceived the AIDS Memorial Quilt; has long been active in Democratic Party and union politics; and is a true hero of mine. When our paths crossed, he was working with UNITE HERE.

Highly respected by the San Diego gay and lesbian community, Cleve ran a very contentious meeting at the UNITE HERE offices between the San Diego LGBTQ leadership, union leadership, and me. He was so good at facilitating this meeting that a compromise was reached. I would get sign-off and cooperation if I were to stage a lunch hour demonstration on the Friday of Gay Pride Weekend. I had wanted to have our rally and demonstration on that Sunday when there were 400,000 people milling about town, and could have used the Saturday parade to hand out fliers and organize people to come to a demonstration the next day, but Pride organizers wanted it on Friday at noon, a far tougher assignment. After a few hours of considering my options, I agreed to compromise and the boycott was born.

The timing was right to ally myself with UNITE HERE, which was very strong in San Diego. When I toured their offices after our lunch and saw several dozen bullhorns in their storeroom, I knew I had the perfect partner. Unions and the LGBTQ community had a history going back to Harvey Milk and a boycott of Coors Beer. And unions stepped up early to fight Prop 8, too. SEIU and the California Teachers Union both made large donations.

For the next several weeks, I devoted all of my time to making the launch a success. I hired Ryan Whitacre, who was going to college in San Diego, to promote the boycott and demonstration. I took photos of the imposing Manchester Hotel towers from every angle and turned the best and most ominous looking one over to a young graphic designer with the suggestion that the word "Boycott" be stamped over the photo. I wanted our logo to be an angry red and black. He did an incredible job. I then had T-shirts, posters, fliers, and a jumbo sign made. Ryan spent the next several weeks going to all the businesses in Hillcrest, the gay neighborhood of San Diego, putting up and handing out fliers.

On Friday night, one week before the demonstration, I planned a "Bar Blitz"—going to all the gay bars and restaurants in San Diego to hand out our fliers. Since there are at least twenty such establishments, it was an ambitious undertaking for one night. But I wanted to make a big splash doing this. I wanted to get the word out and let the LGBTQ leadership know that I was serious. So I hired a stretch limousine for the evening and found six young activists and friends to help.

The blitz was a big success. We hit all the bars over a six-hour period. We all wore the distinctive red and black Manchester Boycott T-shirts. Since we hadn't cleared our plan with the owners and managers, we usually met some resistance as we stormed a place, some of it hostile and some not. But we would accomplish our mission of making known our presence and announcing the demonstration.

At Bourbon Street, a very popular bar, we encountered some volunteers from the local No on Prop 8 campaign there to sign up volunteers. They had asked permission of the owner and blended in while doing their work. We, on the other hand, did not. We stormed the packed bar until we were asked to leave. But by then, everyone in Bourbon Street knew about the boycott and our demonstration. Then it was back into the waiting limo and on to our next stop.

Working with UNITE HERE made a big difference. The union got a lot of its members and supporters to come to the Friday demonstration. Members set up the sound system, had signs and a huge banner made, and did so much more. And they had the resources to sustain the boycott. Local 30 would end up devoting staff and even assigning two interns to work full time dissuading conventions from booking at the Manchester Grand Hyatt.

I had planned to distribute a press release a day before the demonstration. To my surprise and delight, however, I received a call from the *Los Angeles Times* earlier in the week. The paper did a big story on our effort.

That story caught the eye of the *New York Times*. A reporter called, and her story ran a day before the demonstration. It read in part:

> *"Our main beef is the exhaustive amount of money he contributed with glee to take away this brand-new right and to write discrimination into the California Constitution for the very first time," Mr. Karger said.*
>
> *Mr. Manchester said Wednesday: "This really is a free-speech, First Amendment issue. While I respect everyone's choice of partner, my Catholic faith and longtime affiliation with the Catholic Church leads me to believe that marriage should be between a man and a woman."*
>
> *On Tuesday, Brian S. Brown, executive director of the National Organization for Marriage California, a group supporting Proposition 8, sent out an e-mail message warning of the boycott, calling it a "bullying" tactic.*
>
> *Mr. Karger said he planned to expand his protest to include business owners across the country who supported Proposition 8. Though his group will only boycott large donors, he said, the organization will publicize the names of business owners through letters and e-mail messages to customers and by listing their names on the organization's Facebook page.*
>
> *"He and his fellow donors have awakened a sleeping giant," Mr. Karger said of Mr. Manchester.*

Leif Strickland, a former reporter himself, had my favorite response to the article. He told me: "I can't believe it, the *New York Fucking Times*." I couldn't believe it either. The story of my brand new organization, Californians Against Hate, and our warning to contributors to Yes on 8 in the *New York Times*! For the very first time in twenty-eight elections across the country to ban gay marriage, we were fighting back against these hateful bullies, and they now knew it. There were suddenly consequences for those who planned to give vast amounts of money to take away the rights of a minority. We were off and running.

On Friday, July 18, a group of about 200 demonstrators gathered in front of the Manchester Grand Hyatt. I had been worried about turnout—noon is a tough time on a working day—but we had a big crowd of union members, members of the LGBTQ community, local activists, and press. Gilbert Baker, the Grand Marshal of the Pride Parade and creator of the rainbow flag, brought his three-block long rainbow banner. It encircled the hotel.

On the night of our bar blitz, I had met a young woman who had a small band. I hired the group to entertain the demonstrators. And since this was a lunchtime event, we served Subway sandwiches to all. This triggered a memorable line from longtime international gay activist Peter Tatchell, who had flown in from London for San Diego Pride. He was impressed with what we were doing in California and told me that of the over 3,000 demonstrations that he had been a part of, this was the first one where sandwiches were served. "I like to do things a little differently," I replied.

The event was peaceful, although we were met by a small, noisy group of pro-Prop-8 counter-protestors holding nasty signs. The police had cordoned these thugs off, positioning them directly in front of the hotel's entrance. We heard later that Global Hyatt in Chicago was most upset about that. The corporation has spent millions on its corporate image. Now here were twenty fanatics greeting their guests and, worse, being shown to the entire city on the news that night.

On the following day, I ran into Cleve at the Gay Pride festival. "What did you think about the demonstration?" I asked.

"Oh, it was fine."

I sensed some hesitancy. "And how about me? Is working together going to be okay?"

"Yeah, it's fine."

Now I was sure that something was bugging him. Was it that he was a Democrat and I was a Republican? We were going to be working together, so I repeated my questions. "So what do you think, Cleve?

"Did you really do the Willie Horton campaign?" he asked.

Cleve, who is just a few years younger than I am, has these puppy dog eyes. At that moment they were pleading, *Please say no.*

"Yes," I replied. "But there were two. We did the good one."

He turned away, threw his hands in the air, and took off.

"Wait!" I yelled after him. "I'm on your side now."

And we are on the same side. Cleve, the radical Democrat, union organizer, now calls me "Brother Karger" and has endorsed my bid for the presidency. He did so in glowing terms in May 2010 at the dedication of the Cleve Jones Wellness Center in Keene, New Hampshire. And in February 2011, he told the *Washington Post* that I am a "Republican Harvey Milk." These are gratifying and sobering words from a man who knew Milk so well.

As I write this, the boycott continues. Scores of meetings have been cancelled by groups that don't want to spend their money at hotels operated by a man who has demonstrated his disdain for the LGBTQ community. Thousands of individuals and businesses unwilling to cross our picket lines have also stayed away. As a result, the boycott has exceeded our wildest expectations. According to its own admission, the effort is costing the Manchester Grand Hyatt alone approximately $1 million per month. Early on, a high level Manchester executive, who happens to be gay, asked me what it would take to end the boycott. I told him we wanted a like contribution of $125,000 to the anti-Prop-8 effort. Of course, that was a dealbreaker.

***

The Manchester boycott is not our only ongoing action. In November 2008, right after voters approved Proposition 8, we undertook the more difficult boycott of Terry Caster. Caster was the second-largest individual California contributor to Prop 8, giving a total of $693,000—$283,000 to qualify the initiative and $410,000 to get it passed. "Without solid marriage, you are going to have a sick society," Caster had told the *San Diego Union Tribune.*

In July, after his son gave $10,000 to bring the family total to $293,000, we started a "Call Terry Caster Campaign," with a Leif-designed website, a slick logo, and lots of media coverage. We listed his office telephone numbers on the site and in all printed materials. He got so many calls that he made a special recorded message. He chose to spew more hate, and I am sure it helped our boycott.

No more money came in from the Caster family for four months. Then Caster gave that final $400,000 just four days before the election. Slick. He knew that it would not be revealed until the votes were cast.

We weren't going to let that slide. We responded on our website and in a press release with a full boycott of all forty California locations of Caster's A-1 Self Storage. "If you are a current customer of A-1, we hope that you will move your belongings to another company. There are hundreds of other self-storage businesses to choose from. Those who are looking to rent a new storage unit, we encourage you to go to any one the many other options available." Thanks to the mainstream media and the incredibly effective gay blogosphere, word of these and other Californians Against Hate efforts spread rapidly to millions of people.

Our other efforts included two boycotts that ended quite favorably following intensive negotiations. One took place after my press conference in Salt Lake City. I'll describe it in the coming pages. The other took place several months earlier in September and October 2008. Our target? Bolthouse Farms.

You might very well have a Bolthouse Farms product in your refrigerator. The company, started by the Bolthouse family in 1915, is the second-largest producer of carrots in the U.S. It is also known for its health juices, smoothies, protein drinks, and salad dressings sold in upscale stores across the country. In 2005, Madison Dearborn Partners, a private equity firm, bought a majority stake from the Bolthouses for a reported $1.2 billion.

During the summer of 2008, it was revealed that William Bolthouse, Jr., who had run the company for years, had donated $100,000 to the pro-Prop-8 effort through his family foundation. According to its website, the foundation distributed money "to glorify the Lord Jesus Christ by supporting charitable and religious organizations whose ministry, goals, and operating principles are consistent with evangelical Christianity." Apparently the Bolthouses believed that opposing same sex marriage was consistent with their Christian beliefs.

The gay blogosphere was alive with calls to organize a boycott of Bolthouse Farms products. As CAH had just launched its boycott of the Manchester hotels, eyes turned to us. Initially, I was hesitant to go after the company. According to the website, the Bolthouse Foundation was completely separate from Bolthouse Farms. It claimed that it was not funded by the business and that no members of the foundation had a financial interest in the company. When questioned by some of the bloggers, the company affirmed this and distanced itself from the contribution.

My hesitancy began to melt in August when bloggers noted that there were still significant connections between the Bolthouses and the company they had sold. Late in the month, *Wall Street Journal* (WSJ) reporter Tamara Audi interviewed me for an article about the boycotts. She wrote:

> *Mr. Bolthouse has said, "I'm not connected to Bolthouse Farms at all." "But we don't accept that," says Fred Karger, who runs Californians Against Hate, a new gay-rights group that is leading the charge to identify and publicize corporate connections to significant donors. He notes that Mr. Bolthouse's son-in-law is chairman of the company and that Bolthouse Farms markets itself as a fourth-generation company.*

The article scared the hell out of Bolthouse Farms. The Manchester boycott was going well. The food maker didn't want to be next.

Shortly after the piece ran, I received a phone call from a consultant for the firm. He reaffirmed the position of Bolthouse that there was no connection between the company and the contribution to Prop 8. Then he strongly suggested I refrain from boycotting his client. I did consider refraining, but I also did some additional research. In doing so, I learned that William Bolthouse did in fact have an ongoing relationship with the company. He leased over 25,000 acres of farmland to Bolthouse Farms and his son-in-law Andre Radandt was the company's chairman.

The last thing Madison Dearborn Partners wanted was a Bolthouse Farms boycott. The gay dollar is significant, and the firm's portfolio includes many popular consumer-related enterprises—restaurants like Ruth's Chris Steak House, The Yankee Candle Company, Inc., and the Family Christian Store, the largest Christian retailer in the United States. But boycott we did.

On September 19, Californians Against Hate issued a press release that read in part:

> Today Fred Karger, Campaign Manager for Californians Against Hate, sent a letter to Bolthouse Farms Chairman, Andre Radandt, in which he said: 'As of Saturday, September 20, 2008, we will embark on an effort to get the message out to the gay and lesbian community and our millions of friends, family members, neighbors and co-workers all over the United States to 'Don't Buy Bolthouse.'

By now, I knew the drill. The next morning, a Saturday, a dozen or so of my friends and allies joined me in front of the Ralph's Supermarket on Sunset Boulevard (aka the Rock 'n Roll Ralph's). We wore "Don't Buy Bolthouse" T-shirts (black with a red circle and a slash through a bottle of juice) designed by my graphic artist friend Brad Mayo and carried signs reading "Californians Against Hate." (I had already purchased the Internet domain name DontBuyBolthouse.com and Leif designed another great website.)

We set up a table with information and, as an extra draw, free candy. And, oh yes, we marched behind a bagpiper on the sidewalk in front of Ralph's. Note to those of you thinking about organizing a demonstration: a bagpiper definitely draws the attention of passersby. The press covered this, and our second national boycott was born.

We certainly captured the attention of the powers that be at Bolthouse. While we were demonstrating, my lawyer Cary Davidson showed up, all excited. He told me that Bolthouse CEO Jeff Dunn would like to meet with me the next day at the benefit for an organization called the Gay and Lesbian Task Force. I was on the host committee for the event and had helped with fundraising. Now it seemed that Bolthouse Farms would like to purchase a $5,000 table.

I was shocked. The CEO of a billion dollar company, a guy who had been the President of Coca-Cola North America, wanted to meet with me within 24 hours of the boycott announcement. Playing various scenarios in my head, I decided I would ask him for the same thing I'd asked from the Manchester people—a like donation of $100,000 to the No on Proposition 8 campaign to offset Mr. Bolthouse's contribution to Yes on 8.

The fundraiser was a fancy luncheon at the Beverly Hills Hotel. Jeff Dunn couldn't have been nicer. At the event he pledged $5000 of his own money to the No on 8 campaign. He gave me his home phone number and cell phone number and said he was sure we could work something out.

Negotiations began that week. I drew up a settlement proposal that I drafted with my attorney, Cary. But we did not hear back from Dunn. I got the impression that he might be stalling, hoping to drag this out until after the November election. Then it would be moot.

More pressure was needed. On September 27, we held a demonstration in New York on a cold rainy Saturday at the Whole Foods flagship store at Columbus Circle (after determining the store carried Bolthouse products). On Sunday, October 5, we held another demonstration at the Whole Foods near DuPont Circle in Washington, D.C.

The D.C. demonstration took place the day after the big HRC annual national dinner. There, I had passed out fliers promoting the boycott. Dunn was also in attendance.

I was at a table with leading members of the gay media, which up to this point had done a great job of spreading the word about the boycott. No doubt the company I was keeping strengthened my negotiating position. Dunn came over. There was no available chair, so he had to kneel to talk to me. Very awkward. He said he wanted to settle. I said I did, too.

Although the D.C. demonstration the following morning was small (like the other two), it was effective (like the other two). We received some mainstream media coverage, significant gay blogs coverage, and I was able to send out photos and a story to the several thousand folks on my ever-increasing email list. We settled a few days later.

"Carrot firm's olive branch" ran the headline over an article by Maria La Ganga on the front page of the *Los Angeles Times*. An excerpt:

> The "Don't Buy Bolthouse" campaign ended because the company's chief executive "has provided us with a compelling perspective which clearly demonstrates the separation between Bolthouse Farms and . . . its founder, William Bolthouse,"

Californians Against Hate said Wednesday in a written statement.

That perspective, the statement continued, "provides us with confidence that Bolthouse Farms is committed to working productively with the [lesbian, gay, bisexual and transgender] community."

For its part, the Bakersfield-based food giant "thanks Californians Against Hate for recognizing our work to meet our mission of showing respect and integrity to our employees, our vendors and our customers," company spokesman Lane Hudson said.

The article did not mention the terms of our agreement. Bolthouse Farms refused to give money directly to the No on 8 campaign. I knew they wouldn't, but that was my opening position. Instead, the company agreed to give even more than the $100,000 that William Bolthouse had given to Yes on 8, to LGBTQ organizations that could then legally transfer the money to the campaign (with the exception of one $25,000 contribution to the Williams Institute, a think tank on sexuality and the law at the UCLA School of Law). Donations included: $45,000 to Equality California Institute, $15,000 to National Center for Lesbian Rights, $15,000 to Los Angeles Gay and Lesbian Center, $10,000 to Human Rights Campaign, and $10,000 to Parents and Friends of Lesbians and Gays. My attorney Cary did a great job of helping with the negotiations and structuring the agreement. Afterwards, the head of one of the recipient organizations told me, "I like these boycotts. You should do more of them."

I have to say that I'm very proud that we were able to work with and persuade the new management of a business that had been so anti-gay under William Bolthouse to be supportive of LGBTQ organizations. Bolthouse Farms' commitment continues.

The company provides major support to HRC and contributes annually to the Williams Institute and Equality California.

***

You may be wondering how we found out about all the contributions made to the Yes on Proposition 8 campaign. By law these donations must be reported to the California Secretary of State. In turn, that office must make available lists of donors to individual candidates and ballot initiatives in a timely fashion. Anyone can view these lists by searching a database called Cal-Access. From my days as a political consultant, I knew it was essential to "follow the money." Our mission at Californians Against Hate was to out the haters.

The donation monitoring had begun in earnest shortly after the demonstration in San Diego. Brian Wilson, a good friend who is a great detail person and excellent researcher, turned a room in my house into an office and began checking Cal-Access every day for those contributing $1000 or more to Yes on 8. My plan was to find more boycott targets.

In September of 2008, we announced the Californians Against Hate "Dishonor Roll." On a scroll designed to look like old English parchment, we listed the biggest donors—those who gave $5,000 and above. When appropriate, we also dished a little dirt about them—outrageous quotes (such as advocating the death penalty for gays), business affiliations, other organizations to which they contributed, problems with the law, etc. We chose not to publish the contributors' home addresses, even though they are public information and included in the Secretary of State's filings.

The aim was to make our website a destination for the media to find critical information and to answer the question: who are the biggest donors behind the effort to ban same sex marriage in California? I wanted to keep an aggregate of all that the largest contributors were giving, to make it easier for the press. Otherwise it would take hours to go through the reports to total up all that someone had given. I said early on that I wanted to make it "socially unacceptable to give vast amounts of money to take away the rights of a minority." Based on all the whining that the Yes on 8 campaign did about our Dishonor Roll and all the attention that it received, I think I was successful.

I write periodically for the *Huffington Post*. On that site, I announced the biggest offenders as of September 11. The Knights of Columbus of New Haven, CT, the political arm of the Catholic Church, led the way with a $1.275 million contribution. John Templeton, Jr., son of the founder of Templeton Funds, was second at $900,000. He was followed by the National Organization for Marriage (my number one target since I launched CAH); Howard Ahmanson, heir to the Home Savings & Loan fortune; Donald Wildmon's American Family Association; and Elsa Prince, the major funder and member of the board of James Dobson's Focus on the Family.

On that post, I also wrote:

> These mega donations are mostly from out of state organizations and individuals that are pouring money into California to end marriage equality. They are trying to crush us by flooding the state with far, far right money like I have never seen before. They have put these hateful ballot measures before the voters in 27 states, and have won all but one: Arizona 2 years ago. Now this year they are back on the ballot in Arizona, in addition to Florida and California. Their big spending and bullying ways send a terrible message to an entire generation of young people in California and around the world.
>
> These major funders of the Yes on 8 campaign say that the institution of marriage is threatened by same sex marriage.

What harm is the marriage of my friends Scott and Todd causing these people? They are both executives with big companies in Los Angeles who have been together for seven years and were finally able to legally marry. Their wedding and reception was as loving and happy—if not more so—as any of the dozens of straight ceremonies that I have been to.

I am proud to be a Californian, and know that once again we are leading the way. We Californians can hold our heads high with pride, and wonder why so many businesses, people and organizations from far away places are giving so many millions of dollars to strip away equality for all.

We will track this money and publish it on our website for the world to see. If they want to spend tens of millions of dollars to take away our rights, then we will let everyone know exactly who is doing so. Then fair-minded people can decide if they want to spend their hard-earned money patronizing businesses that then turn around and use that money against them.

Initially, the donations to Yes on 8 came in surprisingly slowly. What should have been a money machine appeared to be having trouble. By August, however, the checks started rolling in.

Having been involved in state politics for over thirty years, I figured I would recognize the names of most of the big donors from California. But I didn't. Who were these newcomers?

Brian and I started googling them. And surprise! We found that many of them had several things in common. One, they had attended Brigham Young University. Two, the only other campaign to which they had previously donated was Mitt Romney for President. And three, they lived in Sacramento, Riverside, Oakland, San Diego, Los Angeles—all in close proximity to Mormon temples. BYU, Romney, the Temple. Put them all together and they spell Mormon connection. *Interesting*, I thought. The Catholic Church was somewhat out front in the Yes on 8 campaign through its comments and its contributions from the Knights of

Columbus. But the Mormon Church, although opposed to same sex marriage, did not appear to be playing a central role.

I called Tammy Audi at the *Wall Street Journal* and told her that I had uncovered something big: "Mormons are pouring money into Yes on 8," I said. "No one else really is."

Tammy put me in touch with Mark Schoofs, a *WSJ* investigative reporter also based in Los Angeles. Brian met with him for a couple hours at a local Starbucks, taking him through the Secretary of State's website and our findings. Then Mark, who had won a Pulitzer Prize in 2000, went off on his own. I was dying for the article to appear, because I thought it might slow down the millions of dollars that Mormon families were contributing. (I tipped off the No on 8 forces about the Mormon influx of up to $500,000 per day of contributions to Yes on 8, but apparently they weren't interested.)

On September 20, Mark's story appeared in the *Journal* under the headline: "Mormons Boost Antigay Marriage Effort." I quote portions of it at length here because its explanation of the Mormon Church's coercive tactics, secrecy, philosophy with respect to same sex marriage, and relationship to other religious groups helps explain my future battles with them.

Mormons have emerged as a dominant fundraising force in the hotly contested California ballot fight to ban same sex marriage. Members of the Church of Jesus Christ of Latter-day Saints have contributed more than a third of the approximately $15.4 million raised since June 1 to support Proposition 8.

The Mormon Church decision to enlist members on behalf of the same sex marriage ban has given supporters of Proposition 8 a fundraising lead....

The top leadership of the Mormon Church, known as the First Presidency, issued a letter in June calling on Mormons to "do all you can" to support Proposition 8.

Mormon donors said they weren't coerced. "Nobody twisted my arm," said Richard Piquet, a Southern California accountant who gave $25,000 in support of Proposition 8. He said Mormon Church leaders called donating "a matter of personal conscience." Some Mormons who declined to donate said their local church leaders had made highly charged appeals, such as saying that their souls would be in jeopardy if they didn't give. Church spokesmen said any such incident wouldn't reflect Mormon Church policy....

The Mormon Church encouraged its members to send their donations to a separate post-office box set up by a church member, said Messrs. Schubert and L. Whitney Clayton, a senior Mormon Church official involved in the campaign. Mr. Clayton said the church didn't keep track of how much individual Mormons donated, just the cumulative total. He said members bundled the donations and forwarded them to the campaign.

A Web site run by individual Mormons, Mormonsfor8.com, has tracked all donations to the Yes on 8 campaign of $1,000 or more listed on the California secretary of state's Web site. The site's founder, Nadine Hansen, said they have identified more than $5.3 million given by Mormons but believe that donations from church members may account for far more than 40% of the total raised.

Robert Bolingbroke, a Mormon who lives near San Diego, said he and his wife decided on their own to donate $3,000 in August. Later, he was invited to participate in a conference call led by a high church official, known as a member of the Quorum of Seventy. Mr. Bolingbroke, a former president and chief operating officer of The Clorox Co., estimates that 40 to 60 Mormon potential donors were on that call, and he said it was suggested that they donate $25,000, which Mr. Bolingbroke did earlier this month. Mr. Bolingbroke said he doesn't know how he or the other participants on the call were selected. Church leaders keep tithing records of active members, who are typically asked to donate 10% of their income each year to the Mormon Church.

Same sex marriage hits at the heart of Mormon theology, said Terryl Givens, a professor of literature and religion at the University of Richmond. According to scholars and documents on the Mormon Church's official Web site, couples married in a Mormon temple remain wedded for eternity and can give birth to spirit children in the afterlife. Most importantly, Mormons must be married to achieve "exaltation," the ultimate state in the afterlife. Mormons also believe they retain their gender in the afterlife. "This all explains the Mormon difficulty with homosexuality," said Mr. Givens. In a theology based on eternal gender, marriage and exaltation, "same sex attraction doesn't find a place."

The church, which typically stays out of political issues, has occasionally entered the fray. In the 1970s, for example, it opposed the Equal Rights Amendment.

The prominence of Mormon donors in the Proposition 8 fight has also led to alliances with evangelical Protestant groups and other Christian religions, some of which have deep theological differences with Mormons.

In the weeks that followed publication of this article, more Mormon money flowed to Yes on 8, primarily from California and Utah. CAH hammered home the Mormon connection in a series of press releases. We also added names of Mormons and non-Mormons to our Dishonor Roll. In the end we published the names of over 700 of the 1200 donors of $5000 or more. We would have listed the other 500 contributors, but we couldn't keep up with the flurry of last minute donations.

***

I'm sorry to say that when the initiative to ban gay marriage qualified for the ballot in the spring of 2008, I knew that our Yes on 8 opponents were going to prevail. The same fourteen words in Proposition 8 had been on the ballot in 2000 in California, and we'd lost by twenty-three percentage points. Not too much had happened in those eight years. Yes, the landmark case, *Lawrence v. Texas*, was upheld by the United States Supreme Court, and Massachusetts had allowed gay marriage, but that was about it. This time around, polls showed we might win. But remember, I was in the room when Bill Roberts offered the blunt observation that became known as the Bradley Effect. Voters aren't always honest with pollsters; many people don't want to admit to strangers that they don't support gay rights. Also, there was much confusion about this ballot initiative; a yes vote meant no to gay marriage and a no vote meant yes to gay marriage.

Our side was outmaneuvered all summer and fall until three weeks before election day, when a new campaign team arrived led by Patrick Guerriero, on loan from Tim Gill's political operation, Gill Action, and a whole slew of true professionals finally came in to run the No on 8 campaign. They tried to rescue the moribund campaign. The No on 8 money followed as well, to the tune of $1 million per day. Sadly, it was too late to combat the Mormon-financed commercials, phone banks, and massive door-to-door drives. In the *Huffington Post*, I wrote about how "the Mormon power grab is tearing us apart."

I spent election night, November 4, at the Boom, which had been serving as Democratic Party and No on 8 headquarters in Laguna Beach. All my attention was on Prop 8, but it was difficult to get results. The networks were focusing almost exclusively on the outcome of the presidential race, which was a foregone conclusion. I was actually getting emails from a friend in South America who was getting results before I did. Final Prop 8 tally: Yes 52.24%, No 47.76%. We lost by 599,000 votes.

In several interviews following election day, I said something that I never had said before: I was glad we lost. How could I say that? I explained: "They have awakened a sleeping giant. I know the LGBTQ community is mad as hell and is now going to fight like never before." We came so close, and for the first time we raised more money than our opponents. I wanted to be front and center in the fight to come.

After the election, I looked at the final campaign finance report of the Mormon Church. The Church had reported spending only $2078 on all of its involvement on Prop 8. Crazy! I went to work.

I spent the next nine days holed up in my house and, with Cary's help, put together a comprehensive 62-page sworn complaint against the Salt Lake City-based Church. I filed it on November 13th with the California Fair Political Practices Commission (FPPC). We contended that the Mormon Church had not reported all the money it spent on the successful Proposition 8 campaign.

Eight days later the FPPC announced that it would conduct a full investigation into those charges. And one week after that, I couldn't believe my eyes: the *New York Times* wrote an editorial praising my efforts:

> *Mormons were a major force behind the ballot measure. Individual church members contributed millions of dollars and acted as campaign foot soldiers. The church itself also played an unusually large role. Michael R. Otterson, the managing director of public affairs for the Church of Jesus Christ of Latter-day Saints — the full name of the Mormons' church—said that while the church speaks out on other issues, like abortion, "we don't get involved to the degree we did on this."*
> *Fred Karger, the founder of a group called Californians Against Hate, who filed the complaint, contends that the Mormon Church provided significant contributions to the pro-Proposition 8 campaign that it did not report, as state law requires. The Fair Political Practices Commission of California is investigating, among other things, commercials, out-of-state phone banks and a Web site sponsored by the church.*

In the following chapter, I'll discuss this matter, the Church's retaliation against me, and my continuing fight with National Organization for Marriage (NOM), the front group the

Mormon Church created to do its battles around the country. But now, let's fast forward to that day in February 2009 when I held the press conference announcing the creation of a tip line to learn more about the Mormon money trail (mormongate.com) and my fourth boycott.

The target I announced at my first-ever press conference was the Ken Garff Automotive Group, which owned fifty-six car dealerships in five states. Katharine Garff, the wife of president Robert Garff, had contributed $100,000 to the Yes on 8 campaign just days before the election. "We feel that this huge contribution to take away marriage rights in California by the Garff family warrants a full boycott," my press release read. "The contribution was given very late—on October 29, 2008—and was disclosed in the recently released campaign report."

I arrived in Salt Lake City on a freezing February afternoon. The next day to a packed press conference in a meeting room at the Marriott Hotel closest to Temple Square, I took on one of Utah's most beloved and prominent individuals. Robert Garff had been speaker of Utah State House of Representatives, chairman of the Chamber of Commerce, chairman of the Salt Lake Organizing Committee for the 2002 Winter Olympics, and was currently a member of the Mormon Church's influential Quorum of Seventy.

I was peppered with tough questions for over an hour after my opening statement. I could see my helper Andrew Rhoda, a good friend from Laguna who had recently moved to Salt Lake, shaking his head in disbelief. The assembled press was firing questions at me, but I was making my points, particularly when it came to the Mormon money. We had charts that demonstrated how the Church had underreported contributions and how its representatives had lied. Cary had coached me by phone the night before, so I knew my stuff and after thirty years in the business, I was very familiar with California election law. I made my points and held my own.

During the press conference, a young television reporter said something to the effect of, "I just talked on the phone to John Garff, Robert Garff's son, and he would like to meet with you today. Would you consider meeting with him?"

I think I surprised her. "Absolutely. I'd be delighted."

She paused, then said, "He gave me his cell phone number. Can I give it to you?"

"Yes. I'd be happy to talk to him."

Right after the press conference was over, I called John Garff. A few hours later, I was sitting in his office on the top floor of the Ken Garff Building. To get information about the company and the location of its dealerships, I had previously called and spoken to his secretary. I remembered her name now as she handed me the Garff press release responding to my boycott. She started to leave the office and, right on cue, stopped, turned, and blurted out, "I've been working for the Garff family for thirty-seven years and they're the finest people I've ever known. They would never hurt anybody."

John, about forty, looked embarrassed by the whole matter. He explained that his father was in Palm Springs. In a pleasant, respectful tone, he told me that the company supported gay causes, had given money to HRC, cared about all of its employees, including its gay ones.

I just sat there being courteous, all the while staring at his wedding ring. This was a definitive moment for me. I realized that, nice as he was, this guy was no better than I was. We had just lost the right to marry several months earlier with the passage of Prop 8. Why shouldn't I or anyone else have the exact same rights to marriage that John Garff has?

I also got annoyed when he suggested that his mother had made the contribution strictly on her own; she had not told anyone in the family about it. The Mormons are a patriarchal society. "Really?" I asked. "Your father didn't even know?" He acknowledged that his father had indeed known.

Finally I said, "I assume you wanted to meet with me to settle the boycott. Here's the deal. If your company gives one hundred thousand dollars to LGBTQ groups here in Utah, I will call off the boycott."

John said that business was slow due to the recession. Perhaps they could spread out that amount over five years. *Wow*, I thought. *We can settle this now.* "Four years," I said. He agreed and said to send him a proposal. Knowing the press was waiting to hear about our meeting, we also agreed to say we were in negotiations and had a constructive meeting and other than that had no comment. This was the lead story on the local news that night.

With my lawyer's help, I wrote a proposal that spelled out everything John Garff and I had discussed, including the groups that I wanted to receive the money. Most were in Utah, and all had signed on when I contacted them. They included: the Utah Pride Center, an LGBTQ community center that works with youth; Equality Utah, a gay political organization; and the highly respected New York based GLSEN, the Gay Lesbian and Straight Education Network. GLSEN has gone into thousands of high schools around the country to help set up gay and straight alliances. Its stated mission is "to develop school climates where difference is valued for the positive contribution it makes to creating a more vibrant and diverse community." I figured if any state needed GLSEN's help, it was Utah.

I waited for John's response. Tried to reach him by phone. And then waited some more. John finally called me back and said he hadn't had a chance to look at the proposal. I began to get a sinking feeling that this done deal was not done.

After another week or so, John said he would like to ask Bruce Bastian to be the intermediary. Bruce Bastian! The Utah philanthropist, longtime gay activist, ex-Mormon, who had made his fortune starting WordPerfect, was my hero, a real tough fighter. He had contributed the first $1 million to No on Prop 8 and had challenged other philanthropists to do the same. I'd met him ever so briefly four months earlier in Washington when he had been honored at the annual HRC dinner. Among his many activities, one had stuck out with me: he had taken out billboards all over Utah on behalf of PFLAG (Parents, Families and Friends of Lesbians and Gays) that said, "Someone In Your Family Is Gay." Talk about *in your face.*

It was exhilarating to be in negotiations with Bruce Bastian and John Garff—two of Utah's most powerful men. With Bruce's involvement, we were able to resolve the matter quickly. The Garffs agreed to give the money, said they would change company policy to give partnership benefits to employees, and promised not to contribute to any measure that might be perceived as anti-gay without checking with Bruce. The symbolism of Robert Garff, Mormon pillar, and Bruce Bastian, former Mormon, coming to terms was not lost on anyone in Utah. This was a very successful outcome for a lot of reasons.

On February 27, just sixteen days after my press conference in Salt Lake City, we announced that the boycott was over. My battle with the Mormon Church was far from over, however. Indeed, the same day that I first met with John Garff, I later met with a man whose name I cannot divulge. He gave me a treasure trove of damning information.

Mr. Karger-

I thank you for running. I will be honest, I am hopelessly liberal--but one of the main reasons was growing up with a gay father and then a gay twin brother, and when I became interested in politics there were these two parties. One told me that my family was wrong and that I should be ashamed and disgusted. It told me that as a soldier going to Afghanistan I could fight for America, but my twin could not...

More and more, Republicans are stepping away from their party platform and breaking ranks to support equality regardless of who people are. I think it signals a time when Republicans will not be able to force discrimination on our country because they will not even be able to force it on their own party. What you are doing may end Republican control of anything with the words Christian or family in it. What you are doing will level the field for the next generation of young political hopefuls who will not have to choose between a party that hates their family and one that embraces them, but instead between parties that differ on their approach to education, health care, energy policy and what local governments can and cannot control.

D.

CHAPTER ELEVEN
"YOU GOTTA LOVE FRED'S RACKET."

March 2009. I've been getting under the skin of a lot of people lately. On Christmas Eve 2008, a month after filing my complaint against the Mormons with the FPPC, I received an anonymous death threat. Now, after my publishing of secret documents I was given when I visited Salt Lake City six weeks ago and my filing of a supplemental complaint, two big guns have come out in the open to fire verbal shots.

One is Maggie Gallagher. She is a syndicated columnist, president of the Institute for Marriage and Public Policy and president of the National Organization for Marriage (NOM). I've alleged that NOM poses as an alliance of Catholics and evangelical Christians, but is in reality a front for the Mormon Church. Gallagher has just blogged that my efforts are "part of a broader personal campaign to harass, threaten, and intimidate members of the Latter-day Saints [Mormon] church who exercise their core civil rights to support marriage."

You may want to take what she says with a grain of salt. In that same posting, she has written: "Because the prime argument for gay marriage is an equality argument, [the] traditional view of marriage will also be stigmatized: that is, treated as a discarded and discredited relic of bigotry that we have happily overcome."

(In case you are wondering, yes, this is the same Maggie Gallagher who was revealed in 2005 to have received $41,500 in payments from the Bush administration's Department of Health and Human Services for writing brochures and essays on marriage policy. Nothing wrong with that ... except that at the same time she was writing those brochures, she was praising the Bush marriage policy in her syndicated column. That smells a little, and so does Maggie. And it smells a lot more, when you learn that she failed to disclose those government payments when she wrote her columns on the subject. (When outed, Maggie even acknowledged how inappropriate that was.) So much for the high moral ground.

The other person on the warpath is Brian Brown. He's executive vice president of NOM and is even less charitable towards me than Maggie is. Here is his NOM fundraising letter dated March 20, 2009. I offer it in its entirety because it reveals so much about those who fight so hard to prevent same sex marriage.

Dear Friend of Marriage,
Fred Karger's Wacky Pro-Hate Campaign!
        We just learned we are featured in another Associated Press story this week: Alas for the state of journalism in this country—it's the one in which the nation's most respected news service replays with a straight face the latest wacky charges from a California gay marriage activist named Fred Karger. You gotta love Fred's racket. He files the most outlandish complaints with the California election commission—he knows they are absurd. He also knows the mainstream media will report them with the straight face.
        I first learned yesterday from Google that Fred now has a new charge: National Organization for Marriage is a Mormon front which shows that the LDS church violates election laws somehow. I mean this claim is really silly: If you bother to read the complaint, he points to all the Catholic and Protestant money NOM raised through NOM California to get Prop 8 on the ballot and concludes that the LDS Church is secretly running NOM. And yet this morning on cue, like a dog salivating to the bell, Associated Press runs a national news story about this wacky claim. (No, the AP reporter didn't bother to call us.)
        At least the Salt Lake City Tribune, which ran its own piece on Fred's wacky charges, called me for my reaction. "Outlandish" is the word I used. NOM, as you know, is not a front group at all. We are your voice for speaking up for common sense

on marriage and for defending all of our constitutional rights to speak God's truth to power.

At NOM, people of every race and creed are coming together in love to support marriage. It is truly an extraordinary grace and privilege to work with you. I call Fred wacky but his Orwellian-named "Campaign against Hate" is really hateful. Hate-filled. Fred is not a nice person: He leads the charge to take away people's livelihoods and punish them for personally supporting marriage.

He's also heading up one of the most vile anti-religious campaigns I've ever seen–directed right now primarily against the Mormon Church. First, he attacks the LDS Church because that's a minority faith community... but who will be next on Fred's angry hate-filled blacklist?

It's sad, pathetic and disturbing; and it's also the new face of the gay marriage movement in America. Listen, I'm sure even most folks who support gay marriage are more generous and fair-minded than Fred. But with the Associated Press's eager help, Fred is turning himself into the new face of the gay marriage movement in America: self-righteous, careless of truth, anti-religious, filled with hate for his neighbors who disagree with him and a desire to punish them... and why? Solely because you and I dare to exercise our core civil rights to protect marriage as the union of husband and wife.

That's what passes for hate speech in Fred Karger's world. But with your help, and God's, I promise you: The rest of us in America will never have to live in his sad, strange, narrow world.

I cannot tell you how precious your prayers and your support are to me. God's blessing be upon you and your family, Brian S. Brown

My reaction? Methinks he doth protest too much.

***

So how did it come to this? A chronology is helpful.

On November 4, 2008, the same day that Barack Obama was elected president, Proposition 8 narrowly passed, banning gay marriage in California.

On November 13, on behalf of Californians Against Hate, I filed a formal complaint with the state's Fair Political Practices Commission (FPPC). In a nutshell, we noted that other organizations that had campaigned for Prop 8, such as James Dobson's conservative Focus on the Family, had, as required by law, disclosed non-monetary contributions. Not so the Church of Jesus Christ of the Latter-day Saints (LDS), the Mormons.

Besides raising $30 million of the $40 million for Yes on Prop 8, LDS activities appeared to include phone banks organized in California and Utah, sending direct mail to voters, transporting people to California, using the Church press office to send out releases, organizing mammoth precinct walks every weekend, running a speakers bureau, distributing hundreds of thousands of lawn signs and other campaign material, paying for church leaders' travel to California, setting up slick websites, producing commercials and other video broadcasts, and conducting at least two satellite simulcasts. We noted that while activities related to "member communication" need not be reported, these actions were directed at California's 17 million voters, not just Mormon Church members. Failure to report violated the California Political Reform Act.

We further noted that the only mention of any compliance came in a campaign filing right before the November 4th election, in which the Mormon Church reported non-monetary contributions of only $2,078 for a few small items including Church Elder L. Whitney Clayton's travel expenses for one trip to California. Hard to believe, since the Church made Yes on Prop 8 a national priority beginning on June 20. That's when Church President Thomas S. Monson sent a letter to be read in every church building: "We ask that you do all you can to support the proposed constitutional amendment (Prop 8) by donating of your means and time to assure that marriage in California is legally defined as being between a man and a woman." This was a highly unusual action. As a living prophet, when President Monson speaks, it's God speaking.

Our request to the FPPC concluded:

> On November 9, 2008, Don Eaton, a spokesman for the Mormon Church, was quoted on ABC KGO Television, stating, "The Church of Jesus Christ of Latter-day Saints put zero money in this [election]." When I personally spoke with him Monday, November 10, 2008, and asked him if the PreservingMarriage.com web site was sponsored by the Church, he quickly said that it was not, but was "a part of the campaign."
>
> In 1998, the Mormon Church directly contributed $1.1 million to ban same sex marriages in Alaska and Hawaii, and received widespread criticism for that. So this year in California it appears that the Mormon Church was trying to avoid any direct contributions to Yes on Prop 8, and instead raised millions from its member families. That is legal, but all the money spent to communicate with nonmembers must be reported if it exceeds $100. Clearly the Mormon Church has vastly exceeded that threshold.

On November 21—despite the protestations of the Church, whose chief spokesman termed my allegations "false"—the FPPC sent me a letter that said it was going to launch an investigation into the Mormon Church's activities involving Prop 8. This is rare. The FPPC investigates less than 5% of all complaints it receives, and it had never before investigated a religion.

I got that news via the phone on November 23, when I called the commission from Tupelo, Mississippi. On my way to a vacation in Key West, Florida, I'd stopped in Tupelo—best known as the birthplace of Elvis Presley—to see what I could find out about another organization in the opposition camp, Donald

Wildmon's American Family Association (AFA). The AFA had given $500,000 to pass Prop 8, and I had been tipped off about some of its questionable financial practices. (The AFA is also infamous for calling twenty-five boycotts of some of the biggest companies in America over their support for LGBTQ organizations and boycotting television shows with content it finds objectionable.)

I had a two-hour meeting with the tipster, a former employee, on the day I arrived. The following day, I talked my way into AFA headquarters and got a full-blown tour. I didn't dig up much new dirt, but I got a much clearer understanding of this leading national anti-gay organization. As I was getting ready to leave, a group of AFA staffers formed a prayer circle. We held hands and all prayed.

In my motel room in Tupelo, I wrote a press release trumpeting the FPPC's decision to investigate. I knew it would be a huge news story. On my way to the airport in Memphis the next day, I must have fielded thirty press calls. As I was boarding the flight, the *New York Times* called. The *Times'* Jesse McKinley not only did a story the next day, but that weekend the paper ran an editorial. Titled "The Prop 8 Campaign Money," it read:

> *Based on the facts that have come out so far, the state is right to look into whether the church broke state laws by failing to report campaign-related expenditures.... Fred Karger, the founder of a group called Californians Against Hate, who filed the complaint, contends that the Mormon Church provided significant contributions to the pro-Proposition 8 campaign that it did not report, as state law requires. The Fair Political Practices Commission of California is investigating, among other things, commercials, out-of-state phone banks and a Web site sponsored by the church.... Churches, which risk their tax-exempt status if they endorse candidates, have more leeway in referendum*

campaigns. Still, when they enter the political fray, they have the same obligation to follow the rules that nonreligious groups do.

One month later, on Christmas Eve, I was checking email and found a Google Alert that my name was on Craigslist. I linked to the site and found a threatening post suggesting that my life could be in danger. Since forming CAH I had received a great deal of hate mail, but nothing as frightening as this.

For safety's sake, I always sent copies of the hate mail to a friend of mine to save. Now, feeling in danger, I called the police. Since I opened the email in Los Angeles, I was advised to come to the station in the Hollywood Division and file a complaint. Unfortunately, the policeman at the desk was rude and sarcastic. He asked me what side of Prop 8 I had supported. When I told him, he became even less helpful.

Getting no satisfaction from the LAPD, I called Bill Rosendahl, a friend who is a member of the Los Angeles City Council. He is openly gay and understood the seriousness of the threat. He involved his chief of staff, who contacted a high-level deputy chief. My report was suddenly taken seriously, and I had an excellent meeting with the lead detective in the Hollywood division the next day, Christmas.

While I didn't think an attempt on my life was imminent, I confess to being unnerved and angry. I wanted the perpetrator caught. The case remains open.

NOM and its minions were busy over the holidays. On January 9, 2009, the group sued the State of California in federal court. According to NOM, the law requiring disclosure of ballot-initiative donors was unfair and dangerous because it encouraged and resulted in harassment of contributors.

Mother Jones magazine would later write in a profile piece on me: "It's a serious case from a group of lawyers who have an excellent track record at overturning campaign finance laws. James Bopp (a partner in the Christian right law firm representing NOM) brought the original lawsuit in *Citizens United v. FEC*, the Supreme Court case that in a seismic ruling led the court to throw out federal limits on corporate spending in elections. The California lawsuit could have implications far beyond the state, striking at the heart of more than 40 years of transparency legislation."

Eventually, NOM would subpoena me in this case. More on that later.

Ross Johnson, a staunchly conservative former Republican state senator and then current FPPC chairman, responded to NOM's action by saying that the suit sought "to destroy campaign finance disclosure by a death-of-a-thousand-cuts. I don't intend to let that happen on my watch." Bravo.

Speaking of the FPPC, the Mormon Church had until January 31, 2009, to file its final campaign report on Prop 8 expenditures and amend its earlier reports. There's an age-old political trick of dumping bad news late on a Friday afternoon to try and stay out of the media's eye. Sure enough, on Friday, January 30, 2009, the Church filed a Major Donor Report with the California Secretary of State listing $189,903.58 in non-monetary expenditures on behalf of Protectmarriage.com.

That's considerably more than $2078. How could they have missed that earlier? I've nicknamed my good friend and attorney Cary Davidson, "Cautious Cary." Caution is a good trait for any lawyer, particularly any lawyer representing me, as I tend to be quite aggressive. On seeing this latest campaign report, however, Cary came unglued. "That's crazy," he said. He felt that the Church had still vastly underreported its expenditures. "You can file a supplemental complaint until a ruling has been issued," he advised. I salivated, and we began the process to unravel more missing information.

This was the state of affairs on February 9, 2009, when I went to Salt Lake City. Holding the press conference the next day that resulted in that surprise meeting with John Garff was my primary reason for going to Utah in the dead of winter. But I had something else planned as well: a meeting with the man I can only identify as Mr. X.

The story of this meeting is, in my opinion, far superior to the plot of the "Owen Marshall" and "McMillan and Wife" episodes in which I appeared. I'll start on January 20. In Washington for the Obama inauguration, I was told by a friend (an ex-Mormon) that a friend of his from Salt Lake City was trying to get in touch with me. "He has some documents for you."

My ears perked up. At the beginning of the Prop 8 effort, I had known nothing about the Mormons. I was still trying to learn about the Church—its teachings, how it was organized, and how it spent its money. One thing was clear: the Church always operated in the shadows.

I realized that my friend was talking about a guy who had called me a few times, but had never been in when I returned the calls. I tried him again and got through. He was not specific about the content of the documents, but said they were important, and he would bring them to Los Angeles. In the dark, I said, "I am planning to come to Salt Lake in a few weeks and we can meet up there."

After I left the Garff Building, I walked to the place where I'd arranged to meet Mr. X, the bar in the Hotel Monaco. It was one of the few trendy places in the city. Utah has complicated liquor laws. At the time, in order to buy alcohol at bars, you had to be a member.

Mr. X said he would recognize me. I sat on a barstool and waited. A few minutes later, he approached. We chatted for a while about our mutual friend and other subjects and then he suggested we go to his home. The documents were there, he said. He hadn't wanted to bring all the papers to the bar, and I guess had wanted to size me up first.

He said he needed certain assurances from me before giving me the boxes. He did not want his identity revealed, he said. I promised him anonymity.

Mr. X did not tell me how he came into possession of the documents, some of which had been leaked to at least one newspaper and some people in the No on 8 camp during the campaign, but never published. I have subsequently been able to piece together the story. My suspicions were confirmed when I participated in the filming of Reed Cowan and Steven Greenstreet's amazing 2010 documentary "8: The Mormon Proposition."

Mr. X told me the box contained official Church documents that I would "find very interesting."

"You're giving them to the right guy," I said.

In my hotel room, I thumbed quickly through some of the papers before joining Andrew Rhoda and another friend, John Poole, at a going-away party for a friend of theirs. The hasty run

222

through the documents didn't reveal any smoking guns, and I confess that I wasn't certain there would be any. Wikileaks had previously published one letter that revealed the Mormons had recruited the Catholic Church as a partner in the movement to ban same sex marriage. I figured that was probably the only damning document or else others would have also been published.

Back home in California, I asked Brian to go through Mr. X's materials. A week later, he said, "You have to read this stuff."

Mr. X proved to be the master of understatement. The documents were not simply "interesting." They were explosive.

I could have posted the best documents immediately on our mormongate.com site (after checking with Cautious Cary, of course). But I thought we would get the best mileage if a major newspaper broke the story. After consulting with several people, including my friend, the brilliant political strategist Chad Griffin, I went to the *New York Times*. The paper was interested and assigned a reporter to go through the documents and talk with me. Unfortunately, he was distracted by another story. After a few weeks, he told me he was impressed by the material, but thought it more of a book, not a newspaper story.

A book didn't fit my timetable. I didn't want to wait any longer. I decided to release eleven of the documents myself. Here's what I wrote on mormongate.com that so infuriated Maggie Gallagher and Brian Brown. Credit goes to Brian Wilson, who was the guy who connected all the dots.

The Mormon Church appears to have created the National Organization for Marriage (NOM) in the summer of 2007 to qualify California's Proposition 8 for the November 2008 ballot. They set it up as a Mormon front group, exactly as they did with a very similar organization called Hawaii's Future Today (HFT) in that state in 1995. HFT was established to pass a constitutional amendment in Hawaii to ban same sex marriage. Sound familiar? They have now expanded NOM into seven more states, specifically to fight same sex marriage in those states. We are posting official Mormon Church documents on this web site, dealing with significant Mormon Church actives in Hawaii. These documents show just how the Church operates and they illuminate the replication of the strategy in California in creating NOM to qualify and pass Proposition 8.

And here's what *Salt Lake City Tribune* columnist Rebecca Walsh wrote after the posting:

Documents leaked to Californians Against Hate show in fascinating detail the calculated way Mormon spiritual leaders spearheaded Hawaii's gay marriage fight 10 years ago. The handful of memos from then-Elder Loren C. Dunn to various members of the Quorum of the Twelve Apostles reveal a political machine within a patriarchy of faith:

Richard Wirthlin, not yet a general authority, polled the relative popularity of Mormons versus Catholics. When results showed Catholics had a better image in Hawaii, Mormon leaders decided to stay in the background. They hired a Hawaiian advertising firm, McNeil Wilson, on a $250,000 retainer. They tacked on gambling and legalized prostitution to give the anti-marriage front group "room to maneuver in the legislature" and "broaden our base and appeal," Dunn wrote. They searched for an "articulate middle-age mother" who was neither Mormon nor Catholic to be the face of the campaign.

I'd be remiss if I didn't offer readers here a sampling from the documents, ten of which were written between 1995 and 1998 by Dunn, who at the time was a member of the Church's First Quorum of Seventy. Here are three excerpts from letters he wrote to Neal Maxwell, a member of the Quorum of Twelve Apostles.

March 6, 1996. Subject: Forming and operating Hawaii's Future Today (HFT), the lead organization in pushing for the constitutional amendment to ban same sex marriage (just as NOM took the lead on Prop 8). "One reason I wanted us organized in

Hawaii the way we are is because President [Gordon B.] Hinckley wanted it that way. A coalition is hard to attack ...." Also: "The ideas are introduced, but the Church is not visible."

March 21, 1996. Subject: Keeping church support secret. "... We have shielded previous donors from recognition because of how the funds were used in the preparation of this project, but in the worst case scenario, current donors might be ferreted out."

June 5, 1996. "We have organized things so the Church contribution was used in an area of coalition activity that does not have to be reported."

I have been accused of being obsessed with the Mormon Church and NOM, which I am convinced was the California equivalent of Hawaii's Future Today. I plead guilty. Why? Because that is how any good opposition research guy is effective—you have to be obsessed and get inside the head of your opponents. I am fighting on behalf of millions of lesbian, gay, bisexual, transgender, and queer Americans whom the Mormon Church chooses to demonize. I am determined to get the Mormon Church out of the anti-gay-marriage business.

In 2010, the highly-respected Southern Poverty Law Center (SPLC), which has long done battle with the Ku Klux Klan and neo-Nazi groups, added NOM and several other gay-bashing organizations to its roster of hate groups, explaining, "Generally, the SPLC's listings of these groups is based on their propagation of known falsehoods—claims about LGBT people that have been thoroughly discredited by scientific authorities—and repeated, groundless name-calling."

After California, the fight against same sex marriage moved to seven states in the northeast—Maine, New Hampshire,

New Jersey, New York, Delaware, Rhode Island, and Vermont. NOM stands in the forefront of this effort. The Mormon Church, while not espousing the violence of the Klan, is similar to that organization in at least one regard. It cloaks itself so that its involvement in denying civil rights remains hidden. I'm committed to pulling off the metaphorical hoods and robes and exposing the truth that the Church has tried to hide.

I find it ironic that many in the movement to outlaw same sex marriage vehemently argue that the federal government should not be involved in our lives, that it is up to each state and its legislature to pass laws that affect its own citizens. Yet these organizations come into states and are every bit the outsiders. Aware of this, they hide their involvement and work hard to give the impression that the movement in the particular state is home grown and funded. Baloney.

The more that I learn about the Mormon Church, the more my outrage grows. I learned a lot during the filming of "8: The Mormon Proposition." The movie does a great job of explaining how the Church worked quietly, but effectively, to defeat same sex marriage. "But," as the *Los Angeles Times* said in its review, "its emotional grounding lies in the stories of Mormon families and gay individuals who have been personally affected by the church's position." Stories of families torn apart upon learning that a child is gay, of families who embraced their gay children and lost friends and relatives, of gay Mormons driven to run away from home or commit suicide, and of sexual deprogramming that included electroshock and lobotomy.

I met many of these people with these stories in March of 2009. Aware of my efforts in uncovering the Mormon connection to Prop 8, filmmaker Reed Cowan, an ex-Mormon himself, had contacted me. The California Supreme Court was holding hearings on a legal challenge to overturn the proposition and there was going to be a demonstration that recreated Harvey Milk's famous march from the Castro Theatre to City Hall. There was also to be a candlelight vigil, as there had been after Milk was murdered. Very emotional.

I flew up to San Francisco to meet Reed and be interviewed for his documentary. After doing some filming, thirteen of us—all ex-Mormons except for me—went to dinner. There I got to know Linda Stay, a fifth-generation Mormon, and her husband Steve. Linda's son Tyler Barrick and Spencer Jones had tied the knot in June 2008 after the California Supreme Court had upheld the legality of same sex marriage. Now, after Prop 8, the validity of that marriage was in question. Linda and Steve had become activists in their own right. They had courageously taken on the Mormon Church by delivering thousands of petitions to Temple Square, the Church's headquarters in Salt Lake City, during the Prop 8 campaign. Their reward for being good parents and opposing Prop 8 was ostracism and condemnation from family and fellow Mormons.

I also met Bruce Barton. He had attended Brigham Young University some forty years ago. The story he told was heart wrenching. After hearing accusations that he was "homosexual," university administrators had forced him to undress and watch pornographic films. Electrodes were attached to his body, including his genitals. When he saw something on film that he either wanted to do or thought was a sin, he was to press a button that sent shockwaves through his body.

So, yes, the Mormon Church needs to stop its cruel treatment of LGBT people.

My determination and I traveled across the country to Maine in October 2009. Six months earlier, the legislature there had courageously passed a bill that legalized same sex marriage. Governor John Baldacci had then courageously signed it into law. But, just as in California, NOM was already organized to get signatures to petition for a November referendum on the law.

As in my home state, I started monitoring the campaign filings. *Déjà vu.* Not too many citizens of Maine were donating money to Stand for Marriage Maine (SFMM), the local organization fighting for the referendum. Rather, SFMM was getting all of its funding from NOM and the Catholic Diocese. There was, however, a catch, and we caught it.

Maine law requires organizations that raise more than $5000 for a ballot initiative to register with the state and to report the names of all who donate $100 or more. NOM never registered. I'll let *Mother Jones* pick up the story:

> *Karger suspected that the boycotts had scared donors, and that NOM was trying to funnel their money to the Maine campaign anonymously. Sure enough, he intercepted 79 emails NOM sent out to supporters after the success of Prop 8 in California and found that 16 of them were essentially fundraising appeals for NOM's work in Maine. "Every dollar you give...is private, with no risk of harassment from gay marriage protesters," one promised. Another read, "Donations to NOM are...NOT public information." Armed with those emails, Karger asked Maine election officials to investigate what he called NOM's "money laundering."*

In October 2009, Maine's five-man, bipartisan Commission on Governmental Ethics and Election Practices held a hearing at the statehouse in Augusta to decide whether or not to investigate NOM, brought on my sworn complaint. I wasn't required to attend, but there was no way I would miss this. My request to testify was honored.

In Maine, I was joined by Danielle Avel, a young columnist from Florida whom I had met while doing the Bolthouse Farms boycott. Danielle has become a great friend. She's a go-getter and smart as hell. I won't even try to put this delicately. She is also a hot lesbian, a tiny blonde with a great figure. Having become my junior sleuth on this matter, she wanted an investigation as badly as I did. Stephanie Mencimer of *Mother Jones* was with us. She had just begun to write a profile and wanted to see me in action.

We knew the odds were against us. A staff report had come out the night before the hearing. It recommended against an investigation. This may have been because SFMM had strong ties with the Catholic Church, which was the public face of the effort.

Brian Brown, the then-executive director of NOM was in Augusta to testify, too. He was accompanied by his lawyer, the third-named partner from James Bopp's law firm, Barry Bostrom. At last I got to meet my opponents, whom I'd been battling for over a year and who had just subpoenaed me.

I had prepared a statement before arriving in Maine. On the eve of my testimony, I had to rewrite it after getting new information. For six months I had been pestering NOM to release its federal tax filings, its 990 forms from 2007 and 2008. I had even filed formal complaints against NOM with the IRS. Less than twelve hours before the hearing, I learned from a blogger friend in Asia of all places that NOM had finally posted these long overdue returns on its website. I needed to incorporate this news into my remarks.

The hearing room was packed with representatives from every media outlet in Maine. "I've spent thirty years in politics, managing campaigns," I told the Commission. "I've filed and read literally thousands of campaign reports in probably twenty-five states. I've never seen this type of blatant disregard for election laws."

I turned over all the emails I had collected from NOM, many of which were specifically fundraisers for the Maine election. I had also received direct mail from NOM. This was in response to my ten-dollar contribution to the organization back in June 2008. As distasteful as it was to give them any money, I knew that it would probably result in getting material that might help me bolster my research. Sure enough, NOM's direct mail was different from its online propaganda. It included mail from none other than former U.S. Senator/current presidential candidate Rick Santorum of Pennsylvania espousing what I can only describe as hateful views against the LGBTQ community. Best of all, NOM sent me a slick eight-page newsletter that contained a financial pitch for the Maine election. This contradicted its claim that it was not raising money directly for the election.

When I got to Maine, I realized I should have brought the newsletter as evidence. I called Brian back in California. He went to my house, found the evidence, and overnighted it to me. In Augusta, I made color copies for each commissioner.

I expected a few questions following my testimony, but as Stephanie later wrote, "The commissioners sat in stony silence." No questions. They didn't ask Brown any questions either. I was convinced we'd lost, that the commissioners would rubber-stamp the staff report.

We later learned that at this point in the proceedings, the commissioners were evenly split. Two favored an investigation. Two opposed an investigation. The fifth was undecided.

Enter Danielle. Stephanie and I had driven together to the hearing. Danielle was supposed to be right behind us, but she got lost trying to find the statehouse and came in late. All commissioners' eyes were on her as she walked in the hearing room.

Just as the vote was to be taken, Danielle stood up and said, "I want to say a few words. May I testify?"

Told that testimony was closed, she persisted. "I came all they way from Florida, and I'm sorry. I couldn't find the room." She's so cute, and she knows how to work it.

Thank goodness that in Maine a proceeding like this is somewhat informal. The commissioners let her testify. She did a great job. Then Brown was invited to respond to her. He was awful, and his story was starting to unravel as he sat sweating in front of the five commissioners.

Following a brief discussion, the panel voted three-two to authorize an investigation. To my complete surprise, we'd won. I think Danielle played a major role in swaying the commissioner who was undecided. Also, he held up and read from the color copy of the NOM newsletter I had received. Best ten dollars I ever spent!

It seemed like every television, radio, wire service, and newspaper reporter in Maine was at the hearing. After the decision each of them wanted to speak to Brown and me, Brian first. The NOM leader said he'd be right back and left to make a phone call. I sure would have liked to know whom he called.

When Brown returned, the press swarmed around him. He was really sweating. Danielle and I kept taking pictures of him as he fended off questions.

Next it was my turn. I thanked the commission for standing up to NOM and its threats. Taking questions, I told all I knew about the deceitful NOM.

Here's how Stephanie described the scene in *Mother Jones*:

> *After the announcement, NOM director Brown ended up side by side with Karger among the TV cameras. Karger may be a gay man fighting a movement that considers him an offense to God, but he is first and foremost a political operator. He shook Brown's hand and joked with NOM's lawyer about his impending deposition. Afterward, leaving the building, Karger was buoyant. 'If I had a budget, I'd be dangerous,' he said with a big smile.*

Sadly, a month later the ballot initiative to ban same sex marriage in Maine passed. I take solace in the fact that a federal judge has ordered NOM to release its list of donors to the effort. NOM raised close to $2 million and did not report any of its contributors as required by law—even after being ordered to do so by the state Attorney General and the federal court. Now that's real chutzpah—and it could result in jail time for NOM officials.

I also take great pride in the fact that in June of 2010, after a nineteen-month investigation, the California FPPC found the Mormon Church guilty of thirteen counts of election fraud because it "failed to timely report making late non-monetary contributions" to the Yes on Prop 8 campaign. The amount: $36,928. The fine: 15% of that total, $5,539 dollars. I told the press: "[The fine] seems a little light since [the FPPC] only looked at $36,000 of their contributions, but it's also historic because no church has ever been fined for illegal political activity in California before. In fact, it's unprecedented."

On its website, the Church said that it had "mistakenly overlooked the daily reporting process" during the last two weeks of the campaign.

You don't care about transparency—you and the radical homosexual community want to harass supporters of REAL marriage. I am the Republican National Committeeman for Iowa. As a private citizen and knowing literally thousands of caucus goers, I will work overtime to help ensure that your political aspirations are aborted right here in Iowa. Have you studied our past caucuses—you have NO chance here in Iowa!

Email message of May 26, 2010, to me from Steve Scheffler, President Iowa Christian Alliance; President Iowa Faith and Freedom Coalition; Republican National Committeeman.

CHAPTER TWELVE
"I JUST HAVE TWO REQUESTS."

April 10, 2010. It has been thirty-three years since I became a political consultant. Four years have passed since I came out to the world and started my campaign to save the Boom Boom Room. Two years ago I formed Californians Against Hate (now Rights Equal Rights) to fight against bigotry and for gay marriage. One month ago I told students at the University of New Hampshire (UNH) that I was considering a run for the presidency.

Today, I am about to enter the Marlborough Room in the Hilton Riverside Hotel in New Orleans. The Southern Republican Leadership Conference (SRLC) has convened here this week. It's the second-largest GOP gathering outside of the Republican National Convention; thousands of Republican activists, primarily from fourteen Southern states, are present. So, too, are most of the men and women seeking the party's 2012 presidential nomination and several hundred journalists.

Those running the conference have not exactly welcomed me with open arms. That's okay. Of late I have been reading *The Audacity to Win* by David Plouffe, one of the masterminds behind Barack Obama's successful campaign in 2008. My takeaway from the book can be summarized in two words: Take chances!

In a sense Obama had little to lose by seeking his party's nomination. Neither do I. But just as Obama had a serious reason for running, so do I. My task on this day and in the days ahead is not only to answer the question: FRED WHO? I have to explain FRED WHY.

***

So how does a gay 60-year-old who has never held political office decide to launch a committee to explore a run for president ... as a Republican? A timeline is in order.

The notion of running for president first came to me during the summer of 2008, in the middle of my Proposition 8 activism. I had always wanted to run for office. The only thing holding me back had been ... me; unfortunately, my desire to stay in the closet had trumped my itch to run. In 2008, that was no longer an issue. I was out and proud.

But why the presidency? Fair question. Obviously, you can have the most impact as president. In the best of all worlds, I might have started on the path to that office thirty years ago, seeking local, then state, then national office. But I didn't. I got my education in politics and government, and during my three-decade career, I greatly influenced local, state, and national policy as a consultant, not as an officeholder.

Now I was sixty. I have a lot of ideas for making the country a better place. I can't start at the local level and work my way up. There's not enough time.

I am not a one-issue candidate. However, the issue of LGBTQ equality is of principal importance to me. The timing is perfect, and there is a definite lack of tough and effective leaders out there.

After getting the idea to run for president, I didn't tell a soul for over a year. As you've read on earlier pages, I've been intimately involved in several presidential campaigns. I also know how difficult it is to run for president. First, I had to prove that I was serious and credible. No easy feats.

People would think this was a stunt. I had to show that it was not. This could be accomplished by hard work, creativity, and determination. Demonstrating credibility would be a lot tougher. I would need to get a tremendous amount of attention, do everything right, present myself well, and have a lot of good old-fashioned luck.

As the year progressed, I felt like I was making headway on this score. I don't claim to be a one-man band, but I was the leader of a small band that was able to get a lot of bang for a few bucks. As I told Stephanie from *Mother Jones*, I'd be even more dangerous if I had money.

As I've written, in January 2009 the National Organization for Marriage and Protect Marriage.com filed a federal lawsuit challenging the constitutionality of the campaign finance disclosure provisions of California's Political Reform Act. Saturday morning of Labor Day weekend eight months later, I was sitting on my upstairs deck in Laguna Beach with good friend Eric Siddall when I heard the doorbell ring. I got up and looked down at a stranger.

"Fred Karger?" he asked. I nodded. I had a sick feeling. Then he said, "You're served."

The subpoena I was given required me to appear for a deposition on October 13. I also had to produce all emails, financial records, communications, and documents going back to January 1, 2008—nearly two years of records!

James Bopp was identified as NOM's attorney. Eric, who is also an attorney, Googled him on my computer. "Oh my God!," he screamed. "This guy's incredible! He's got an 80% success record in front of the [U.S.] Supreme Court."

"Thanks for that good news," I said as I dialed Cary in a panic. Actually, I had anticipated something like this for some time. I knew I couldn't be as aggressive as I was without some repercussions.

Matt Pordum of the *Los Angeles Daily Journal* broke the story, writing:

> *"This is harassment and they are trying to silence me,' said Karger, who points out that he's not a party to the case. 'I'm a citizen activist, and my organization is just me, funded entirely by myself versus the power of a group who has millions and millions of dollars behind it."*

With just fourteen days to respond to the subpoena, Cary assigned a litigator from his firm to frame a response. Meanwhile, I looked for a high-powered lawyer to go head-to-head with the Bopp firm, its co-counsel the powerful Alliance Defense Fund, and their deep-pocketed clients. I called my distant cousin, David Levi, for a recommendation. Before becoming Dean of the Duke Law School, David had been a federal judge. In fact, he'd been chief judge in the Sacramento district in which the NOM case had been filed.

When I explained to David what had happened, he said, "Here's who you should use: Matt Jacobs." Matt, a partner in the Sacramento-based firm of Stevens, O'Connell & Jacobs (which has since merged with DLA Piper), was the right guy—dialed in, political, and smart.

Not surprisingly, the firm was also expensive. To help pay my anticipated fees, I created a legal defense fund—something I'd hoped I'd never have to do. But I knew I had to raise some money. I also wanted to see if I had built up enough good will around the country with all of my activism to fundraise for the first time.

With good friend Andrew Reynolds, I came up with the concept "Five for Fred" one night in Laguna when a group of us were out. We sought small contributions from large numbers of people. I would ask for five dollars, the price of a Starbucks latte, plus tip, to help me fight back against NOM.

It worked. I raised almost $20,000 with just one email appeal and great coverage of my subpoena from the incredible LGBTQ media and bloggers. Many supporters took the fund's name to heart and sent five dollars.

In addition to helping cover legal bills, this showed me that I had a national reach to raise some money if I decided to run for president. Political fundraising has changed dramatically in recent years. Thanks to the Internet, a well-written appeal can now raise millions. Over the last few years, I've found that my cause is helped every time I'm attacked—whether by a hateful organization like NOM or a bigoted individual like Steve Scheffler from Iowa.

When I was trying to save the Boom, many of the leaders in the gay community had their doubts about me. I think they thought I was crazy for doing so much to try and save a gay bar with a funny name. That skepticism only increased during the Prop 8 battle. I don't think that any of the long-established LGBTQ organizations were happy to see me playing the Lone Ranger. But when NOM started sending out nasty letters and then subpoenaed me, my relationship with the movers and shakers in the gay community took a dramatic turn for the better. For the first time, I think they felt sorry for me and realized the value of what I was doing. Some even came through with contributions to my legal defense fund for far more than five dollars.

In November 2009, I shared my presidential aspirations for the first time. My sounding board was Matt McCarty, my personal trainer, physical therapist, friend, and quasi-shrink—a "one stop shop," I call him. Matt, a bright, liberal 30-year-old with a strong interest in politics, has been helping me with bad neck problems since 2005. He's always been interested in my adventures and has been especially enthusiastic when I've gone after the establishment.

Hearing my own words, "I'm thinking of running for president," gave me pause, made me question my own sanity. But Matt got it. He understood my motivation and what I could accomplish by taking my activism up a few notches.

While I didn't exactly need Matt's blessing to undertake the run, I did want my family's support. Most often a potential candidate weighs the pros and cons with spouse and kids. I had neither. But I did have a brother, sister-in-law, niece and nephew, and my cousins with whom I am very close. If they had serious objections, I wanted to know.

My brother has a beautiful second home in on the Big Island in Hawaii. He invited me to come for Christmas 2009. My cousin Butch Karger, who is like a second brother to me, and his wife Nancy would be coming, along with their two kids and two of their grandchildren—thirteen Kargers in all. This seemed the perfect time to drop the P (for President) bomb.

Before leaving Los Angeles, I confided in a few friends, including Cary, who at first just rolled his eyes. I asked these confidantes how they thought I should share the news in Hawaii. Should I clink a glass at dinner and make the announcement to all?

Or should I tell Dick first? The consensus was: talk to Dick in private, then to the other eleven or so in attendance.

On the first night of my visit, I joined my brother after dinner on the lanai that overlooked the ocean and the famous Mauna Kea golf course. It was a beautiful tropical evening. Dick was smoking a cigar. The last time I'd said I needed to tell him something was when I'd come out of the closet nearly twenty years earlier. He'd been very supportive. Now, he told me that running for president was the craziest thing he had ever heard. He was right, but I knew that. He peppered me with questions about why I was running and what issues I would talk about.

Soon Dick's son Rob joined us. "You're never going to believe what Fred's thinking of doing," Dick said. "If you took a million guesses you'd never get it."

Rob shrugged. "I don't know. Run for president?" Apparently our mutual friend Shane, whom I had told in L.A., had shared the news with my nephew (who obviously knows how to keep a secret).

Rob and his sister Nicole were enthusiastic about the possibility. Butch and Nancy, who had previously sent a generous contribution for my legal defense, were also supportive. Over the next four or five days, we often talked about my "crazy" plans.

After returning to Los Angeles, I brought in detail man Brian Wilson, who had done such great Prop 8 and Dishonor Roll work. We put together a test-the-waters trip that would take me to Washington, D.C., New York, and New Hampshire, site of the all-important first-in-the-nation primary that follows the Iowa caucus.

Before leaving on this trip at the end of February 2010, I spoke to some gay activists in Los Angeles. At a dinner, I ran into

Chuck Wolfe, head of the Victory Fund, a D.C.-based organization that provides monetary support to openly gay and lesbian candidates. He said, "We're not going to support you."

No surprise. I had never held elective office, was a Republican, and was thinking of running for the highest office in the country. I didn't think he'd jump for joy. I asked him to keep an open mind and suggested we talk again when I was in Washington. He agreed to set up a meeting for me with Deputy Political Director James Dozier, who works with the Republicans the fund supports.

When I reached D.C., I found James friendly. He went through the list of standard questions for prospective candidates. None really applied to someone running for president.

Next I met with Matt Brooks, executive director of the Republican Jewish Coalition, a group of which I've been a member for a long time. He had a look of disbelief throughout our meeting at his office. After stressing my family's heritage of activism beginning one hundred years earlier, I noted that in addition to being the first openly gay candidate to ever run for president, I'd also be the first Jewish Republican to run (save for a brief effort by former U.S. Senator Arlen Specter in 1996).

Among the other people and groups that I visited in Washington: Kellie Ferguson and Bethany Vensel of the Republican Majority for Choice, another organization I've supported for decades. Also Michael Komo, a student who headed Allied with Pride, a gay-straight alliance at George Washington University. That group had been in a flap with the school's College Republicans a few weeks earlier over the appearance of gay-friendly Meghan McCain on campus.

These were not "Will you endorse me?" meetings. I was simply doing my due diligence—getting acquainted with the major players and seeking their advice. In politics, you want to go and talk to people first and make them a part of the process.

With LGBTQ leaders I would sometimes say that our "fierce advocate," President Obama, had been a disappointment and that it was important to expand our reach to the Republican side of the ledger. But I wasn't pushing hard. My standard line was: "I just have two requests. One, please try to keep an open mind. And two, watch what I do." I would not ask for anything. I had to prove that I was serious and would strive to become credible.

It's always wise to leave something behind so folks will remember you. Everyone I met received press kits, which included some of the articles from my Prop 8 work and my resume. I also gave away little pins that I'd had made up. On one side of the pin was the American flag; on the other side was the gay rainbow flag.

Naturally, everyone was skeptical. "Why start at the top?" they asked. "Are you going to be a one-issue candidate?"

Though understandable, the skepticism of most of the influential gay and Republican leaders was discouraging. Fortunately, I had been reading about my hero Teddy Roosevelt and took some comfort in his experience. At the beginning of the twentieth century, his fellow Republicans hated him. He was too progressive for them, and they tried to stop him every step of the way. Similarly, courageous African-American Congresswoman Shirley Chisholm faced huge obstacles in her bid for the Democratic nomination back in 1972. I knew this trip was going to be uphill all the way.

In D.C., I went to a fascinating debate at the Cato Institute between political commentator and author Andrew Sullivan, NOM'S Maggie Gallagher, and British member of Parliament Nick Herbert. It was moderated by Cato Executive Vice President David Boaz. Topic: Is there a place for gay people in conservatism and conservative politics?

This was the first time I had ever seen Gallagher in person. What a disaster! When she wasn't speaking, she sat babbling to herself. I took lots of great pictures of her for later use.

Next stop: three days at the storied annual meeting of the influential Conservative Political Action Conference (CPAC). I met up with Danielle and we made the rounds. We went to some of the presentations, spent a lot of time in the exhibition hall, and heard several of the possible 2012 candidates for president speak. We also talked about what it might be like when we returned to CPAC the next year. Where would I be in twelve months?

New York was more discouraging than Washington. The winter weather was brutal and responsible for some of the gloom. I was supposed to meet with David Mixner, who has remained a leading gay activist since those days of the Briggs Initiative. But wind and freezing rain led to cancellation of this and other meetings.

My cousin Dave Karger, a senior writer at *Entertainment Weekly*, was going to drive me from New York up to New Hampshire. We were to visit 97-year-old Mimi Karger in Peterborough. She's Dave's grandmother and my aunt. I also had plans to speak at some college campuses and meet with some of New Hampshire's political movers and shakers.

On the way north, we stopped in Westchester County to have brunch with Dave's parents, Mary Jane and Tom. Dave's brother Mike and his wonderful wife Sarah were also there with their new baby Ellie. Dave is also gay (I think it runs in the family!), and his boyfriend Todd Jackson is another great addition to the family.

When Dave came out to me about fifteen years ago, he sought my advice about coming out to his parents. I rarely give counsel on that difficult decision, but knowing all the parties, I gave Dave the thumbs up. When he came out to his parents, it went very well.

Mary Jane, a school social worker, quickly became the most incredible gay activist mom. She has done so much and helped so many. She has served on the national board of GLSEN for a decade and has been a big booster of everything I've done.

Due to the storm, the power at their home had been out for several days. But thanks to a back-up generator, Mary Jane was able to make an incredible brunch. At the table, we talked about my possible run for president. I was clearly ambivalent.

As Dave and Todd and I were leaving, Mary Jane took me aside and asked me what I was going to do.

"I don't think I'm going to run," I said.

Mary Jane looked up at me with her big brown eyes. "You've got to," she said. "We need leadership. There's no one." Her appeal was powerful and had a huge impact on my eventual decision. But it wasn't until a few nights later, when I gave the speech reprinted at the beginning of this book to the Gay-Straight Alliance at the University of New Hampshire, that I decided to go for it.

After overnighting at Dave and Todd's weekend home in Connecticut, Dave and I took off bright and early Sunday morning for New Hampshire. We met Aunt Mimi and her family in Peterborough for another family meal at her granddaughter's wonderful Mexican restaurant. Then we drove Mimi back to her assisted care facility. She's the last link to my parents' generation and a special lady. It's hard to see her so frail, but what a life she had. Her spirit shines through. I thought of my mom and dad and wondered what they would think of all this.

Dave dropped me off at the Jack Daniels Motor Inn. (Really!) The next day I rented a car and drove to Concord, the capital. There, the Centennial Hotel would be my home for the next five days.

After a day of meetings in Concord with a variety of Republicans, I headed over to UNH in Durham. I had a wonderful meeting with Dante Scala, Dean of the Political Science Department. He bought me a coffee and offered advice and recommendations of others with whom I should meet.

Then I went to the regular Tuesday night gathering of the Gay-Straight Alliance. That meeting changed my life. The students let me speak for fifteen minutes. I told my story for the first time, and boy did they react.

It was in that small basement room of the MUB (Memorial Union Building) with forty kids—most of them sitting on the floor—where I first knew that I was doing the right thing. These young people were so awed by the fact that someone who was gay could run for president that I decided then and there to go for it.

The following night I drove up to Hanover and met with a small group of students in the Dartmouth College Gay-Straight

Alliance. They were just as excited by the prospect of a gay guy considering running for the highest office in the land. Throughout the week, I received lots of emails and Facebook messages from the college students I'd met. The stories these young people shared were moving and persuaded me I'd made the right decision.

During that first trip, I set up several other meetings with various politicos, academics, LGBTQ activists, and Republican leaders, including the then-executive director of the New Hampshire Republican Party, Andy Leach, and party communications director Ryan Williams.

In New Hampshire, people take you seriously when you say you're thinking about running for president. When you add that you are a gay Republican, they pay extra special attention. Several other relatively unknown candidates have succeeded there before. (I think that I could do well in the New Hampshire primary, now set for February 14, 2012. The state is a good fit for a moderate Republican; 42% of voters are registered Independents.)

When I got back to California, I asked Brian Wilson to come back to work for me. He's my rock—a great friend, a huge talent, and a good generalist. He can do most anything. Next I brought recent Georgetown graduate Kevin Miniter on board part time to help with the research. He and I had met several months earlier at a Los Angeles fundraiser for the No on Amendment 1. That was the Prop 8 campaign of 2009 in his home state of Maine. He liked what I was doing with CAH and had volunteered to help. I had given him a couple of research assignments, and he'd proven himself to be one smart guy. I now had my team in place.

Before heading to the Southern Republican Leadership Conference in New Orleans, I went to Iowa. There, One Iowa, the state's largest LGBTQ advocacy group, and Lambda Legal were hosting a big fundraising dinner celebrating the first anniversary of the Iowa Supreme Court's unanimous seven-zero decision to allow same sex marriage, something no longer allowed in my state. (Sadly, in November 2010, all three of those seven Iowa justices up for reconfirmation were ousted by voters energized solely by that one decision.)

Before the dinner in Iowa, I had lunch with Kevin Miniter's friend Keenan Kautzky and Keenan's boyfriend Darren Jirsa. They were so nice, and later that evening they introduced me to practically everyone in Des Moines. I met several of the seven wonderful couples who had been plaintiffs in the court case. And surprise, after meeting several political leaders at the dinner—all Democrats—I met a Republican.

Joy Corning had served two terms as lieutenant governor. She was pro-choice and had been a board member of Planned Parenthood. I was so excited to meet a Republican who supported marriage equality that I asked her to have lunch the next day.

There is probably no less hospitable arena for an openly gay candidate than the Southern Republican Leadership Conference. And that's one reason I went from Iowa to New Orleans. Announcing that I was considering a run for president would make news there. With Sarah Palin, Ron Paul, and others expected to attend, I knew the press would be out in full force.

Years in the consulting business taught me that a campaign is a bit of a show. It's important not to be wandering around the conference by yourself. I wanted to impress, demonstrate that I had a team in place. My entourage included Danielle, Kevin, my film documentarian John Keitel, and Chris

Morrow, my producer for CNN's iReport project. Thanks to meeting Chris in Sacramento in January of 2010, I have continued to document much of my campaign in iReports. This project engages citizen journalists to upload video shot on flip cams and iPhones to CNN's website.

The conference took place at the Hilton Riverside. Weeks earlier I had contacted the organizers and said I would like to use the press room for a press conference to announce that I was considering running for president. "That room is only for conference speakers," I was told.

Now when I called the Hilton to see if I could reserve a meeting room (as opposed to the press room) for a press conference, I was asked if I was part of a group or convention. When I fessed up, the hotel sales rep said she would have to check with the SRLC. The organizers again said, "No."

Knowing that this was my first test of getting turned away and having to fight my way in, I drafted a hard-hitting letter of protest. I copied Cary on it and included his law firm's website. The letter was addressed to conference director Chuck Davis. I followed up with several phone calls, none of which were returned.

I was determined to have my kickoff press conference in a traditional meeting room. I guess I'd had in the back of my mind what my press conference would be like if I ever ran for office—the room, the banner, the podium, press kits, coffee, and everything laid out.

An end-around was necessary. I asked Danielle to reserve a Hilton meeting room under her name. At the same time, I rented a parlor suite—not ideal for a press conference, but a good backup. The SRLC could not control that, as it was considered a hotel room and was booked through general reservations. If the meeting room Danielle had reserved was off limits, I'd use the parlor suite to make my announcement.

We waited until the day before my announcement, April 9, to hand out the press release. I wanted to do this at the last minute, thinking that the SRLC organizers would be so busy that they might not try and stop us.

Kevin and Danielle and I went to the press room and all the different receptions and we passed out the releases. I even gave one to Michael Steele, then chairman of the Republican National Committee, when we ran into him that night in the Hilton Executive Lounge high atop the hotel.

The press release was headlined: "First openly gay candidate to announce for president." He read it, slapped me on the shoulder, and said, "Excellent, you're mixing it up."

Indeed. But was the SRLC going to send security in the morning and shut me down?

No. At 10 a.m., I stepped up to the podium in the meeting room to begin my press conference.

This book begins with a speech, and so it shall end with one:

I am strongly considering becoming a candidate for President of the United States in 2012. I would run as an Independent Republican, and would likely be the only true outsider in the field.

I did not come about this decision lightly. It would be a serious undertaking.

I would be an unconventional candidate, and if I run, I will wage an unconventional campaign.

I want to help determine the direction of this country and, in the process, work to redefine the Republican Party.

I would be the first openly gay candidate to seek the nomination of a major political party as its Presidential candidate.

My thirty-five years of experience as a fighter in politics places me in a unique position to run. I have worked on nine presidential campaigns; this would be my tenth. I have managed dozens of other campaigns all over the country, and would bring that wealth of experience to my own candidacy.

I would build a credible campaign, and would strive to engage and register new and younger voters. My campaign would be highly strategic, and utilize the latest in digital media technology to attract volunteers and raise the necessary funds.

I would discuss issues important to the gay and lesbian community. I will work hard to end Don't Ask, Don't Tell; pass the federal Employment Anti-Discrimination law (ENDA); eliminate the federal Defense of Marriage Act (DOMA); make gay marriage the law of the land; and make finding a cure for HIV / AIDS and a vaccine to prevent HIV a new national priority.

My positions and ideas on other issues will be forthcoming. I will work quickly to surround myself with the best and brightest experts. I will address the important issues: the economy and job creation, America's wars in Afghanistan and Iraq, homeland security, health care, the deficit and education.

Our nation is facing many challenges right now. We need new and creative leaders to solve them.

I will work tirelessly to bring back the spirit in every man, woman, and child to help remake America the land of opportunity and equality for all.

Shirley Chisholm captivated the nation when she ran for President as this country's first serious black and female candidate in 1972. Her campaign paved the way for Jesse Jackson's Presidential campaigns in 1984 and 1988, and the election of Barack Obama as our forty-fourth President in 2008.

A new chapter in American history begins in New Orleans today.

That night I threw a catered party with an open bar in my parlor suite (couldn't let it go to waste). About one hundred people attended over the course of the evening, some from the convention, some just random hotel guests. A cute blonde woman came up to me and said, "I have to meet Fred Karger." She introduced herself as deputy director of the SRLC. She had been the bearer of bad news every time I had asked for anything from the conference.

"How did it go?" she asked.

"Great," I said. "But hey, what happened? Why the change of heart? I didn't think you'd allow me to hold my press conference."

She told me that when her boss received my letter and saw that I had copied my lawyers, they realized they might have a problem if they tried to stop me from speaking.

Bingo. My plan had worked. I had taken on the SRLC, the largest Republican gathering in the country after the Republican National Convention, and won. This was an important lesson for me. I realized that if I was going to get anywhere over the next two years, I'd have to fight and claw my way in.

If I am not officially invited to the party ... I guess I'm just going to have to crash it.

Index of Names

Made in the USA
Lexington, KY
29 February 2016